TV and Caricature

TV And ...

Series Editor(s): Amy Holdsworth, Karen Lury

TV and Cars
Paul Grainge

TV and Caricature
Hannah Andrews

TV and Caricature

Hannah Andrews

EDINBURGH
University Press

Edinburgh University Press is one of the leading university presses in the UK. Publishing new research in the arts and humanities, EUP connects people and ideas to inspire creative thinking, open new perspectives and shape the world we live in. For more information, visit www.edinburghuniversitypress.com.

© Hannah Andrews, 2026

Grateful acknowledgement is made to the sources listed in the List of Figures for permission to reproduce material previously published elsewhere. Every effort has been made to trace the copyright holders, but if any have been inadvertently overlooked, the publisher will be pleased to make the necessary arrangements at the first opportunity.

Edinburgh University Press Ltd
13 Infirmary Street, Edinburgh EH1 1LT

Typeset in in 12 on 14pt Arno Pro and Myriad Pro
by Cheshire Typesetting Ltd, Cuddington, Cheshire, and

A CIP record for this book is available from the British Library

ISBN 978 1 3995 0808 7 (hardback)
ISBN 978 1 3995 0810 0 (webready PDF)
ISBN 978 1 3995 0811 7 (epub)

The right of Hannah Andrews to be identified as the author of this work has been asserted in accordance with the Copyright, Designs and Patents Act 1988 and the Copyright and Related Rights Regulations 2003 (SI No. 2498).

EU Authorised Representative:
Easy Access System Europe
Mustamäe tee 50, 10621 Tallinn, Estonia
gpsr.requests@easproject.com

Contents

List of Figures   vii
Acknowledgements   ix

1. Introduction   1
   The shop window   1
   What is televisual caricature?   4
   TV and Caricature   17

2. Framing Televisual Caricature   19
   Introduction   19
   The address of televisual caricature   21
   Margaret and Donald: The multiple faces of televisual caricature   31
   Conclusion   61

3. Making Televisual Caricature   63
   Introduction   63
   Spitting Image and industrial change in the 1980s and 1990s   66
   Spitting Image rebooted   86
   Conclusion   104

4. Cancelling Televisual Caricature   107
   Introduction   107
   Blackface impersonation and racist (televisual) caricature   109
   A pineapple on his head: The legacy of a blackface televisual caricature   120

Afterlives of televisual caricature: Apologies and
    archival absences   133
Conclusion   144

5. Conclusion   147

References   158
Index   177

Figures

1.1 James Gillray, *Very Slippy Weather*, 1808 © National Portrait Gallery, London — 2
1.2 Crowd watching television set in store window – Jacksonville, Florida. Courtesy of State Library and Archives of Florida — 3
2.1 Donald Trump trains a legion of impersonators to replace him for everyday tasks, *Our Cartoon President* — 35
2.2 Margaret Thatcher presented as a rusting automaton, *Margaret Thatcher: Where Am I Now?* — 37
2.3 Margaret Thatcher (Michelle Gomez) caricatured via Hannibal Lecter in *Psychobitches* — 42
2.4 Donald Trump (Alec Baldwin) directly addresses the American public in a parody of a presidential speech, *Saturday Night Live* — 45
2.5 Phillip Schofield and Holly Willoughby's 'corpsing' sets a playful tone for their interview with 'Donald Trump' (John Di Domenico) — 52
2.6 Baga Chipz caricatures Margaret Thatcher as a monstrous grotesque, *RuPaul's Drag Race UK* — 57
2.7 The Vivienne's caricature of Donald Trump replicates the president's signature facial and bodily gestures, *RuPaul's Drag Race UK* — 59
3.1 The 'Vegetables' sketch, *Spitting Image* — 65
3.2 Exchequers sketch, *Spitting Image* — 71
3.3 The Queen Mother makes her first appearance on *Spitting Image* — 76

3.4 *Spitting Image* puppets appear on *Top of the Pops* to
     promote 'The Chicken Song'   82
3.5 Donald Trump discovers he has accidentally
     subscribed to Britbox, *Spitting Image* (2020)   88
3.6 Jeff Bezos, Elon Musk and Richard Branson engage in
     a new space race, *Spitting Image* (2020)   92
3.7 Boris Johnson struggles to integrate with 'woke'
     students, *Spitting Image* (2020)   98
4.1 Ann Lee watches images of her husband portrayed
     as a caricature, *Cutting Edge: Footballers' Wives*   127
4.2 The Jason Lee caricature, as shown from Ann's point
     of view, *Cutting Edge: Footballers' Wives*   127
4.3 *Bo Selecta* caricatures the star image of Craig David   135
5.1 Munya Chawawa performs a parody of Craig David's
     'Fill Me In', May 2020   153
5.2 Donald Trump transformed into a deepfake
     caricature in *Sassy Justice With Fred Sassy*, 2020   155

Acknowledgements

Many thanks are owed to a great number of people who have supported my journey towards the production of this book.

The research for the third chapter was funded by the British Academy / Leverhulme Trust Small Grants fund, 2021 Round (SRG21/210915). The book was conceived and commissioned during a secondment at the Institute for Social Responsibility, Edge Hill University. Many thanks to Jo Crotty for her support there. It was completed during research leave funded by the College of Arts, Humanities and Social Sciences at the University of Lincoln. Thank you to Holly Harrod for her support.

Huge appreciation is owed to interviewees, whose insights and memories were influential in my account of the making of *Spitting Image*. These were: Roger Law, Peter Fluck, John Lloyd, Jon Blair, Steve Nallon, Jan Ravens, Kate Robbins, Doug Naylor and Charles Denton. I am also grateful to Deidre Amsden. Sebastian Cody's kind help was instrumental in this process. John Sandy-Hindmarch provided invaluable research assistance on this project and was a pleasure to work with.

Thank you to the staff of the various archives I visited to work on Chapter 3: the Syndics of Cambridge University Library, the staff of Bournemouth University Library Archives and Special Collections, Media Archive for Central England, British Film Institute Library and University of Lincoln Library.

Thank you to colleagues at Edge Hill, who were there for the beginnings of the project: Elke Weissmann, Perelandra Beedles, Claire Parkinson, Ruxandra Trandafoiu and Owen Evans. Thanks to colleagues at Lincoln who have been there at the end: Andrew

Elliott, Gábor Gergely, Diane Charlesworth, Hannah Spaulding, Christine Grandy and Jeongmee Kim.

Thank you to Karen Lury and Amy Holdsworth, who have been behind the project from day one. Thank you to Kelly O'Brien and Gillian Leslie at Edinburgh University Press.

Text from *The Fruit of the Spirit Is Love (Galatians 5:22)* is reproduced with the kind permission of Marvin Thompson and the Poetry Society.

Some research from Chapter 2 has been previously published in: H. Andrews, 'Distorted Recognition: On the Pleasures of Televisual Historical Caricature', *Screen*, 60(2) (2019) 280–97, and 'Drag Celebrity Impersonation as Queer Caricature in The Snatch Game', *Celebrity Studies*, 11(4) (2020) 417–30.

Some research from Chapter 3 has been previously published in: H. Andrews and G. Frame, 'Cancel Culture: The Decline of Political Comedy on British Television in the Early 2020s', *Comedy Studies* (2025), https://doi.org/10.1080/2040610X.2025.2463773, and H. Andrews, 'Transnational Television Caricature: The Global Spread of *Spitting Image* 1984–1994', *Historical Journal of Film, Radio and Television* (2025), https://doi.org/10.1080/01439685.2024.2447139.

This book is dedicated to Greg and Elliott, my family, my team.

1
Introduction

The shop window

What has caricature, the art of rendering individuals recognisable via comic deformation, got to do with television? One answer may be found in an 1808 James Gillray engraving, *Very Slippy Weather* (Fig. 1.1). The setting for this artwork is the street outside a print shop in St James's, London. It belonged to Hannah Humphrey, the exclusive vendor of Gillray prints. In the foreground, we see an unfortunate man grimacing as he slips on ice, while his hat, wig and the contents of his pockets escape him. This spectacle is observed only by a little dog in the corner of the frame. The other depicted figures' backs are turned away, their attention consumed by the shop window, through which they survey an array of Gillray's work. In this public space, caricatures are on display, offering the gathered crowd both a distraction from their immediate circumstances and a means by which they come to know important figures of the day. This crowd is all male, but it is made up of people from a range of social backgrounds, signified by their costuming in tricorn hats, military regalia or ragged clothing. Through this motley collection of rapt consumers, Gillray implies that caricature is a social leveller and a demotic form of visual culture. *Very Slippy Weather* provides an intriguing glimpse into the function of the caricature in the early nineteenth century: a public and popular means of representing political and social elites. In this depiction of a collective gaze at a medium of public

Fig. 1.1 James Gillray, *Very Slippy Weather*, 1808 © National Portrait Gallery, London

communication through the window of a shop there are intriguing parallels with the common image in the mid-twentieth century of crowds gathering outside the windows of electric appliance stores to watch as events unfold through television screens (Fig. 1.2).

Both caricature and TV have been conceived of as tools of civic communication, as means of disseminating the kinds of public 'knowledge' that is shared by a citizenry about political and social structures and the people within them. The circulation of such discourses aided the development of the 'public sphere', Jürgen Habermas's term for the spaces in which citizens, through rational discourse, could reach the reasoned consensus he considered essential for a functioning democracy. Caricature, as visual satire, offers what James E. Caron (2021) calls a 'supplement' to this, a 'comic public sphere' that operates as a parodic counterpart but nevertheless works to sharpen the critical tools necessary for

Fig. 1.2 Crowd watching television set in store window – Jacksonville, Florida. Courtesy of State Library and Archives of Florida

civilised debate. Television has also been viewed as an essential medium in the twentieth- and twenty-first-century public sphere, not only by delivering the kinds of information necessary for democracy to function, but by disseminating cultural representations that impart a sense of the meaning and value of citizenship on a more affective level. Jim McGuigan (2005, 2011) describes the latter as the creation of a 'cultural public sphere'.

A further commonality is the evanescent encounters we tend to have with both TV and caricature. They are cultural forms assumed and often intended to speak to everyday, localised realities.[1] They are ephemeral by design, though, as the longevity of Gillray's caricatures attests, this does not preclude their images from also being embedded in the longer-term cultural consciousness or memory. Both forms have conventionally been designed for immediate visual impact because the anticipated encounter between viewer and medium is not the contemplative 'gaze'

---

[1] This applies more to broadcast television than to TV on-demand. I argue, though, that the space occupied by TV in the cultural imaginary is still substantially connected to its quality of immediacy.

associated with the normative viewer of art, but instead a momentary 'glance'. Of course, the distinction between the gaze and the glance is familiar in media studies thanks to the influential work of John Ellis, whose *Visible Fictions* (1992) established these as the dominant distinction between the modes of viewing for cinema and television.

Very Slippy Weather's presentation of caricature in a shop window reminds us of another shared characteristic with TV: both are modes of representation that operate in a commercial context. Neither caricature nor television emerge from a vacuum of artistic intention; TV is content designed and delivered by and for a complex creative industry. Kiene Brillenburg Wurth argues that caricature shops operated as 'public screens', that 'facilitated a space of social interaction' (2011, 127). For Brillenburg Wurth, these are spaces where 'public personae crystallized in the popular imagination' and therefore 'it is tempting to see in these shop windows a glimpse of the TV screen as it were to evolve out of radio, telephony, the theatre and the visual arts' (2011, 127). In this book, I give in to this temptation. I explore how caricature has been translated from a mode in visual and comic art to a form of televisual representation by looking at the form and context of comic impersonation on television. I analyse this both as extension of a longer history of caricature as a representational form and in the context of television as a medium and industry. This book offers a critical analysis of what I am calling 'televisual caricature'. First, though, allow me to offer some definitions.

What is televisual caricature?

While this book represents the first extended examination of caricature in television studies, it has enjoyed scholarly attention in several other fields, including political science, communications, anthropology and literary studies. It has been of especial interest in two areas. Art historians have examined its place among other forms of portraiture, tracing its origins in ancient Greece, through Italian Renaissance experiments in comic portraits, to Georgian England, where it is generally agreed to have developed as a form of visual satire. Caricature's popularisation through print culture in Western Europe and the United States in the nineteenth and early twentieth centuries saw it converge with other forms of comic art, especially cartooning (Gombrich and Kris, 1940; Feaver, 1981; Lucie-Smith, 1981; Donald, 1996). In facial recognition psychology, the 'caricature paradox' has been studied. This is the curious process by which caricatures render a face recognisable despite, even *through*, its distortion (Mauro and Kubovy, 1992; Lewis and Johnston, 1998). Psychologists are interested in what this might suggest about how humans recognise faces more generally.

The most useful summary definition of caricature I have found comes from psychologist Gillian Rhodes, who explains that:

> The essential features of caricature [are] exaggeration and individuation: a caricature differs from a realistic portrait by its deliberate distortion, and from a grotesque by its representation of a known individual. Other features also commonly associated with the concept are a caricature's power to reveal true character or personality, its focus on defects, its humour, and simplification. (1996, 13–14)

For me, and throughout this book, caricatures are understood to be humorous depictions of real people who are made recognisable through the exaggeration of aspects of their likeness. These are often, but not always, satirical, using these deformations as a means of moral critique of some aspect of the public persona of their target. Caricature's key artistic claim is to use these distortions as a means of externalising the supposedly 'true' or 'essential' personality. Televisual caricatures adapt this practice for the medium of television, whether that is in animation, puppetry or the exaggerated comic impersonation of real people across various genres and modes.

Underlying this definition and the cultural role of caricature are a series of conceptual contradictions. First, caricature depends on simplification, the reduction of the subject to a limited number of exaggerated physical features that are supposed to capture the complexity of the individual. Caricature relies a great deal, therefore, on the cultural knowledge of the perceiver to fill in the gaps. It demands a level of perceptual agency or sophistication on the part of the viewer that can sometimes be overlooked. Second, caricature is usually intended, explicitly or implicitly, to denigrate its target, via distortions of their image and (in its satirical use) moral critique. Yet, by crystallising and exaggerating the public persona, it can simultaneously operate as a curious form of endorsement. Caricature can elevate its subjects into figures 'worthy' of such representation and emphasise personal qualities that may be read not as flaws, but as attributes. Third, caricature, like satire, is frequently seen as subversive in its use of graphic art as a means of ridiculing powerful elites. As with other humorous forms, it can also be conservative, as it polices social boundaries and upholds cultural norms. Fourth, caricature is an inaccurate, antimimetic depiction of its subject, but one that has a necessary relationship to reality, and, for some scholars, to essential or inner 'truth' (Gombrich and Kris, 1940). It therefore operates in a liminal space between fact and fiction. Finally, there is the caricature paradox mentioned above, that the form's exaggerations do not impede and, in fact, facilitate the identification of a subject, a phenomenon I have previously termed 'distorted recognition' (Andrews, 2019). It is these tensions that make caricature such a fascinating object of study, which, in combination with the complex medium of television creates a rich seam for exploration. I will return to these contradictions throughout the book. For now, let's develop a working definition of televisual caricature, drawing on four key themes: individuation, satire, humour and grotesquery.

Individuation

One of the founding figures of the art of caricature, Annibale Carracci, is thought to have said the following about the purpose of the form:

Is not the caricaturist's task ... exactly the same as the classical artist's? Both see the lasting truth beneath the surface of mere outward appearance. Both try to help nature accomplish its plan. The one may strive to visualise the perfect form and to realise it in his work, the other to grasp the perfect deformity, and thus reveal the very essence of a personality. A good caricature, like every work of art, is more true to life than reality itself. (qtd in Gombrich and Kris, 1940, 11–12)

For Carracci, caricatures are simultaneously true and false – indeed, they express truth *through* falsehood.

E.H. Gombrich and Ernst Kris argue that the portrait function of caricature is central to its identity, such that 'a caricature reveals its true sense to us only if we can compare it with the sitter, and thus appreciate the witty play of "like in unlike"' (1940, 13). Caricatures, in this view, are only effective if we can recognise their target. In other words, caricatures individuate.

There is not total agreement on the importance of individuation for caricature. Rebecca Wanzo, for example, describes caricatures as 'fantastic depictions' that are 'not necessarily recognizable likenesses of people' (2020, 4). Embryonic forms of caricature found in the art of ancient Greece and Rome depicted grotesque types rather than individuals (Lucie-Smith, 1981). Proto-caricatures in Italy and France acted more as physiognomic experiments than replications of specific faces (Gombrich and Kris, 1940). Georgian English caricature often prioritised moral allegory over individual critique (Donald, 1996). In common usage, the term 'caricature' frequently conveys (implicitly negatively) distortion through simplification and exaggeration, and operates interchangeably with another derided form, the stereotype. The negative reputation of caricature and stereotype derives from their reduction of the humanity of the subject(s) portrayed to a small number of unflattering tropes or characteristics. The distinction between the modes rests on the matter of individuation: whereas stereotypes imply the (improbable) sharing of a limited number of traits among members of a social grouping, caricatures exaggerate features to render a specific subject recognisable.

Televisual caricature (like caricature found in animation and cinema before it) expands on the capacity of portrait caricature to depict – and deform – individuals by adding movement and voice. Most depends as much for recognition on the quality of the vocal impression as it does on physical appearance. 'Impression' suggests a sketch, outline or simplification that nevertheless has a mimetic function, and may therefore feel intuitively connected to the methods of caricature. This is not, however, a book about television impressions or impressionists. Panel show *The Imitation Game* (ITV, 2018) provides a useful illustration of the distinction, as I see it, between impressions and caricatures. In this programme, professional impressionists compete against each other in a series of challenges based around the skill, whether providing a comic voiceover for archive footage, or delivering quick-fire, one-word impressions to rapidly identify a subject. The show demonstrates the impressionist's ability to balance accurate vocal imitation with comic exaggeration, using skills analogous to the caricaturist. However, impressionists remain visibly themselves, and the pleasure, as in all comic impressions, is in the incongruous, lightly uncanny experience of hearing a familiar voice emerge from the wrong body. Televisual caricature takes this one stage further by including the 'body' in the imitation, adding visual exaggeration to the comic performance. I use 'impersonation' instead, to convey the combination of voice and body. Performers of TV caricature come to embody their subject, however temporarily.[2] The term 'impersonation', like 'caricature', carries cultural baggage. It has negative associations with dishonesty, the illicit attempt to pass oneself off as another person, and, in relation to acting, with surface-level imitation instead of deep engagement with character. An impersonator nevertheless identifies and reproduces core elements of a persona, and a comic impersonator exaggerates these to make the subject more recognisable (and funnier), just as a caricaturist does.

---

[2] This is somewhat complicated in the case of animated or puppet caricature. In these cases, the media combination of voice acting and the 'performance' of animator or puppeteer construct the impersonation.

Colin Seymour-Ure argues that political cartoonists deploy 'tabs of identity' to aid recognition of the subject (2003, 244).[3] These are selective personality elements and easily recognisable visual markers that quickly communicate who is the subject of the image, and together form a 'caricature signature'. This requires analysis both on the part of the caricaturist and of the perceiver, who must make use of an interpretive toolkit to decode the images that they see. James Sherry (1987) argues that portrait caricature, despite its surface simplicity, assumes a level of 'knowingness' in its perceiver: knowledge of the subject's image, because without this, a caricature is merely a character type; knowledge of the norms of portraiture, as this distinguishes between a caricature and a sketch; and knowledge of the reputation of the subject, necessary so that the implicit critique (however gentle or affectionate) can be understood. Televisual caricature similarly requires these three elements to function: a target who is well known enough to be simplified to a caricature signature; an obvious divergence from television's normative representational techniques; and reference (generally topical) to the persona, behaviour or actions of the subject. Its capacity to use exaggeration as critique has led to caricature being seen as a variant of satire.

Satire

Satire is notoriously difficult to define – to the extent that some critics have questioned the necessity of definitions altogether (Condren, 2012). It has been characterised as a 'mode' or 'cluster concept' by scholars seeking to establish parameters for interpretation

---

[3] The distinction between cartoon and caricature is blurry, and the terms are sometimes used in place of one another. As Seymour-Ure notes, cartoons too create likenesses through 'exaggeration, distortion and simplification' (2003, 242). My emphasis on individuation means that, for me, caricature carries a more specific meaning than cartoon, but insights from the study of cartooning are often applicable and useful in the analysis of caricature.

(Greenberg, 2018). The broad consensus is that satire entails the use of wit or ridicule to attack vice or folly (Griffin, 1994). Satire can function as a social regulator, using comic exaggeration to scrutinise ethical flaws with a 'corrective aim' (Hutcheon, 2000, 56). Political satire especially is conceived as a check on power. Laura Basu (2015), for example, suggests that, in response to failures in the fourth estate, television satire has become an important means by which politicians are held to account. James E. Caron identifies television satire as an instrument of the 'comic public sphere', one which 'critiques persisting moral sentiments involving undesirable behaviors such as greed, vanity and moral corruption, behaviours that should be expunged in favor of moderation, empathy and ethical if not moral behaviour' (2021, 58). Political caricature similarly intends to 'debunk[] and downgrad[e]' power, which Lawrence H. Streicher contrasts with advertising, concerned instead with 'prestige inflation' (1967, 433).

Satire and caricature's effectiveness in mitigating the influence of elites has been questioned on the grounds that, instead of wounding the powerful through ridicule, they can provide a helpful platform on which public prominence can be built, to the extent that 'politicians are schooled by their media experts to project themselves as caricatures' (Feaver, 1981, 36). Caricature's ability to identify impactful, repeatable characteristics that aid in the recognition of an individual is aligned with the processes involved in the successful construction of a personal brand. Bal et al. (2009) identify the spoofing of political brands as central to the contemporary practice of political satire and caricature. Of course, the facility with which such brands can be parodied speaks to their success in garnering recognition. Satire and caricature's paradoxical effect is to elevate as well as to denigrate because it offers to public figures a precious resource in the economy of politics: attention. Because the television screen is 'one of the most popular spaces for public exchange and … a place where hegemonic discourses are reified and maintained' (Jones, 2015, 34), its role in this process is magnified. For many politicians, the risk of their image being subverted in satirical critique is worth the reward of enhanced prominence.

Alongside its moral purpose, satire's key defining feature is its mockery of real people, events or situations, as Hutcheon (2000, 104) puts it, 'bringing the "world" into art'. 'Mock' has a dual meaning, connoting both artificial imitation and ridicule, both of which are in operation in satire (Greenberg, 2018, 10). Satire deploys the methods of fiction to reference reality obliquely. The reader or viewer of satire must hold the contradictory position of recognising the real referent in the satirical object, while also engaging in the necessary suspensions of disbelief associated with the consumption of fiction. The referentiality of caricature also renders it 'intrinsically ephemeral' such that it 'loses impact ... when we have nothing at stake' (Wechsler, 1983, 317). The indirect reference to real-world happenings or figures mean that external context is required for a viewer to interpret satire and caricature. But such references are also temporally specific, topical to the time in which the satire is created and harder to interpret once this immediate context has moved into the past (Greenberg, 2018). Television's capacity for immediacy remains one of its assumed special characteristics, although most television is not, now, encountered as live broadcast. Satire's topicality renders it, in theory, a neat fit with the broadcast television medium, since both aim for currency. Yet, as Jonathan Gray et al. (2009, 6) point out, satire television also flourished in the post-network era, in which TV was no longer dominated by appointment viewing and the needs of scheduling. The fit with post-network television hinges on the demographic targeting of a niche audience of value to advertisers, that is, a relatively young, high-income, well-educated group assumed to be the most likely consumers of politically engaged content. The industrial expediency of this audience group and its putative relationship with televisual caricature will be returned to throughout this book.

Televisual caricature is only one of a range of ways that television satire presents its analysis of contemporary reality. Some television programmes, such as *Dead Ringers* (BBC Two, 2002–7) or *The Windsors* (Channel 4, 2016–) deploy comic impersonations as their primary method of critique, while others, such as

Saturday Night Live (NBC, 1975–) or *Tracey Breaks the News* (BBC One, 2017–18) intersperse their caricatures among other sketch formats. Much as not all television satire is televisual caricature, not all televisual caricature is television satire. As this book demonstrates, it appears in a wide range of television modes and genres, including advertising, light entertainment, game shows, children's television and magazine programming. Whether or not the explicit purpose of a televisual caricature is for the conventional aim of satire, to correct moral failure, it nevertheless shares the means of satire: exaggeration, distortion and, above all, humour.

Humour

While satire has subversive potential to the extent that it aims to delimit the authority of social elites, its restatement and policing of normative social boundaries can be viewed as fundamentally conservative. For example, caricature adopts physiognomic critique as part of its satirical arsenal, a dubious alignment of physical imperfection with moral failure that hardly speaks to a progressive worldview. Terry Eagleton expands this analysis of the tension between subversion and conservatism to encompass not only satire, but humour more broadly, which he argues can 'estrange and relativise the norms by which we live, but it can also reinforce them' (2019, 137). Questions of the political status of humour and its 'true' purpose – to maintain or to break the status quo – are present in each of the three major hermeneutics under which it has been analysed, the 'superiority', 'incongruity' and 'relief' theories.

The 'superiority theory' holds that laughter occurs when we feel ourselves to be 'intellectually, morally, or physically above' a person or situation (Stott, 2005, 176). Discussions of this theory tend to cite as an originating idea Thomas Hobbes's identification of laughter as 'a sudden glory arising from some sudden conception of some eminency in ourselves by comparison with the infirmity of others or with our own formerly' (qtd in Stott, 2005, 178). According to the superiority theory, humour is a tactic to be used in a power game, where the joke-teller (or comic equivalent) asserts their strength against the joke's 'butt'. The extent to which humour is seen as subversive or conservative may therefore hinge on who the players in this game are perceived to be. In comedy circles, this is widely described as the distinction between 'punching down' and 'punching up', the former being humour used to denigrate those in society with little power, the already marginalised, and the latter the targeting of someone of social status equivalent to or higher than the joke-teller. In both cases, the superiority theory assumes, following Aristotle's famous assertion that humour is a 'kind of abuse', that joking can be used as a weapon, and that the humiliation associated with being the target of comedy is far from a trivial matter. Caricature largely lampoons social elites, such that Sigmund Freud located its 'charm' precisely in this ridicule of the powerful, 'simply because we count rebellion against authority as a merit' (1976, 149). The targeting of caricature subjects assumed to be protected by their social status against its weaponisation of humour is central to legitimising its cruelty towards the individual.

The 'incongruity theory' locates the essence of humour in the surprising juxtaposition of seemingly incompatible elements. Immanuel Kant's (1914, 223–4) discussion of laughter as 'an affection arising from the sudden transformation of a strained expectation into nothing' is foundational to the theory. The idea of a 'strained expectation' suggests a normative baseline from which the comic situation deviates. While therefore having subversive potential, by detailing imagined breaches of the social order, humour also delimits such possibility, by identifying these breaches as impossible or absurd. Noël Carroll suggests that 'comic amusement, according to the incongruity theory, presupposes that the audience has a working knowledge of all the congruities – concepts, rules, expectations – that the humour in question disturbs or violates' (2014, 27). In the case of caricature, these 'congruities' might be the expected norms of human behaviour and physicality, both of which are distorted for humorous purposes. Other 'norms' that caricature plays with are the conventions available for the representation of individuals in its medium, whether that is expectations of mimesis in portrait caricature, or naturalistic performance in the case of televisual caricature.

Eagleton argues of comic incongruity that 'humour happens for the most part when some fleeting disruption of a well-ordered world of meaning loosens the grip on the reality principle', and that it provides a moment in which the ego can let go of its 'grim-lipped insistence on congruence, coherence, consistency, logic, linearity and univocal signifiers' (2019, 89). This concept of humour as a temporary release from the pressures of everyday existence is often described as the 'relief' theory. Eagleton's use of psychoanalytical terms 'reality principle' and 'ego' is not accidental here: the relief theory's key text is Freud's *Jokes and Their Relation to the Unconscious* in which he argues that jokes can provide momentary release from repressed psychic energy. Humour, according to the relief theory, also provides a socially sanctioned forum in which usually taboo subjects can be aired. Caricature – and political comedy more broadly – similarly provides a permitted means by which elites can be mocked but stands outside the realm of real power or influence. Relief theory also explains the strong connection between comic amusement and bodily abjection. Comedy provides a sanctioned space in which the ordinarily repugnant or offensive – defecation, copulation, disease, injury, death – can be represented at a safe remove from everyday experience. The work of comedy to defamiliarise and to deflate importance can neutralise the potential psychic threat of the abject or uncanny. For caricature, this most often manifests in its (re)construction of the human as grotesque.

Grotesquery

Grotesque representations display disturbed physicality, the violation of laws of nature through distortion, decay, excess or hybridity. In forcing a confrontation with that which is ordinarily repressed, the grotesque connects with the uncanny, as well as presenting 'an embodiment of the abject' (Stott, 2005, 87). Like the comic, the grotesque works to define the 'normal' by envisioning the abnormal. Justin Edwards and Rune Graulund parallel the grotesque's tendency towards exaggeration with the same impulse found in caricature, arguing that 'the exaggeration of the already oversized body part can produce a caricature that will be far more grotesque than the person being represented' (Edwards and Graulund, 2013, 67–8). Caricature expresses its grotesque excesses as comic rather than horrifying, though the line between these in practice may be paper thin. In the case of televisual caricature, the comic framing of the grotesque may help to excuse the appearance of that which is usually unsanctioned on the medium.

Andrew Stott's (2005, 91) brief discussion of caricature in his critical introduction to comedy emphasises the potential of the form not only to render its subject monstrous, but to highlight the potential monstrosity in all of us. This is because the guiding principle of caricature is to make its subject identifiable via the deformation of their facial and bodily characteristics; as Rudolf Arnheim puts it, 'caricature is a spectacular demonstration of expression by deviation' (1983, 320). In this sense, caricatures seem intrinsically paradoxical. The question of how caricatures render subjects recognisable despite – in fact, via – such deformation is what has interested facial recognition psychologists. Faces are especially difficult to recognise, because they are 'complex, multidimensional stimuli', comprising both a set of relatively homogenous features – the same component parts in roughly the same arrangement – and yet each face offers a unique variant (Rhodes, 1996, 115). One theory suggests that we depend for recognition on identifying the elements of how each face diverts from a norm or average, with these diversions then stored in our memory's 'face space'. Caricature may be recognisable because it exaggerates these norm-deviations, the features we use to recognise faces (Rhodes, 1996, 131). Caricatures can, according to Rhodes, in special cases have a 'superportrait' effect, rendering their subject *more* recognisable than a straightforwardly mimetic representation can.

Facial recognition approaches to caricature highlight an important set of concerns related to their cultural role. If caricature representations exaggerate the identifiable elements of a face to prompt recognition in individual memory, how might this work in relation to cultural memory? Caricatures may match up to the persona or public image of famous individuals, exaggerating the traits or features that have been (tacitly) collectively agreed as the subject's identity markers to form a caricature signature. I have elsewhere described this process as 'distorted recognition' (Andrews, 2019). This phrase highlights the dual pleasures for the viewer of caricature: first, the enjoyment of the surprising, witty or outrageous distortions of the human body and face, the 'satirist's skill in representing … deformity' (Griffin, 1994, 166); second, the gratification of identifying the subject of the caricature, the 'delight of decoding' (Griffin, 1994, 167), the satisfaction in knowing that you are 'in' on the caricaturist's joke.

Televisual caricature's employment of 'distorted recognition' raises important questions about the fit of the form with TV. What level of deformation – both in terms of the limits of grotesquery and the acceptable extent to which individuals are lampooned – can be tolerated on the medium? TV occupies a privileged position of attention-gathering and influence in the public sphere, and therefore has a special responsibility to both those who watch it and those who are represented on it. Caricature's deformations are at recurrent risk of spilling into defamations, with potentially lasting consequences. And, in a medium which 'yoke[s] together mass, diverse groups of people … called an audience' (Mills, 2009, 16), how can the recognition of the caricature's subject, so crucial to its pleasure and moral purpose, be guaranteed? These questions speak to the way in which caricature is framed when it appears on television, how television's conventions can be adapted to caricature's methods and aims, and how caricature works as TV content made by a complex creative and commercial industry.

TV and Caricature

An exploration of these tensions in caricature and their alignment with the medium of television has helped me arrive at a working definition of televisual caricature, which I propose as: a mediated humorous impersonation of a real person that renders them identifiable by exaggerating known aspects of their public persona, often though not always with satiric intention or effect. This working definition of televisual caricature allows for it to be distinguished from other forms of impersonation, such as dramatic portrayal or vocal impression. The stress on impersonation also means it will not focus on all instances caricature appears on television, for example as onscreen illustrations in non-fiction programming. The book will expand on this definition by examining caricature in three overlapping conceptual and contextual frameworks. Chapter 2 considers the relationship between televisual caricature and TV address in the context of television's position as a medium of the cultural public sphere. Drawing on work in television studies, media studies and cultural studies, it examines the form of televisual caricature, applying these theoretical ideas to a comparative case study of two persistently caricatured public figures: Margaret Thatcher and Donald Trump. It looks at a range of television contexts in which caricature can be found, from the translation of drawn caricature into animation, use of caricature impersonation in sketch comedy, and in the less predictable spaces of magazine, news or reality TV programming. Chapter 3 looks at caricature's place in the TV industry in two periods of technological, cultural, political and economic turbulence, the 1980s and the 2020s. It does so with reference to a TV show that is unavoidable in any discussion of televisual caricature, the puppet sketch show *Spitting Image*. A hit for Central Television in the 1980s and 1990s, *Spitting Image* expanded beyond British screens in the extra-televisual proliferation of the brand through merchandise, public appearances and exhibitions of the puppets. It returned in 2020 as content for video-on-demand service Britbox, though lasted only two series. Through a combination of archival research, content analysis and practitioner interview, the chapter explores why this might have happened, considering the commercial implications of caricature as television programming or content. Chapter 4 attends to the legacy of televisual caricatures by focusing on a negative use of the form, blackface impersonation. It examines how, in the aftermath of a racist murder in May 2020, historical instances of blackface televisual caricatures were revisited, rebuked and redressed via both public apologies and the removal of this content from publicly accessible TV archives. The chapter evaluates the politics of these content withdrawals and considers what this might suggest about the meaning and value of televisual caricature as a part of television history. Through these examinations of televisual caricature's aesthetics, industrial function, and cultural politics, the book considers it both as a critical development in the ongoing history of caricature as a popular, public artform, and as an overlooked but important, intriguing and sometimes troubling element of television programming.

2

Framing Televisual Caricature

Introduction

Imagine switching on the TV and encountering the image of a middle-aged white woman, with perfectly coiffured strawberry blonde hair, pastel eye make-up and red colouring on downturned lips, wearing a blue suit, carrying a handbag, speaking slowly and deliberately in a soft, low voice. Or a large man with an orange tan and white skin around his eyes, a huge blond bouffant, wearing an oversized suit and long red tie, talking brashly and loudly through pursed lips. How long does it take to recognise Margaret Thatcher or Donald Trump? How long to notice that the hair is a little too large, the make up a little too much, the voice not quite right, the whole thing is ... off? How long to realise that you are *not* seeing Thatcher or Trump, but a comic exaggeration? This happens almost instantaneously. In a mere moment, the televisual image and sound have offered a wealth of cues that communicate first, who this person is, and second, that this is not them – and that is funny. It takes only seconds to frame a televisual caricature.

This chapter nuances the characterisation of televisual caricature offered in the Introduction; that is, as a mediated humorous impersonation of a real person that renders them identifiable by exaggerating known aspects of their public persona, often though not always with satiric intention or effect. I do this via an examination of how caricature is framed using televisual conventions and affordances. I begin by assessing the address of both television and caricature. I compare the viewing practices associated with each, outlining intriguing parallels between the ways that they address an assumed audience. Address currently occupies a quiet place in studies of television, replaced on one side by an audience-centred understanding of meaning and value creation, and on another by close critical readings of television texts. As this section will explore, though, televisual caricature utilises key elements both of caricature form and television's medium specificity to communicate its ideas about its subjects. Caricature and television share the need to appeal to the glancing attention of the beholder, a person who cannot be assumed to have a concentrated look; to construct a disposition in the viewer, drawing on a (proposed) shared worldview; and to convey information about the subject rapidly, depending on a sophisticated but immediate set of interpretive codes necessary to understand and enjoy the representation. These are discussed in the context of caricature's position as a 'citizenship genre', and television's importance as a medium of the cultural public sphere.

I then apply these concepts to a comparative case study that explores televisual caricatures of Thatcher and Trump. Because this is not a book of political theory or history, I have relatively little to say about the real politicians, aside from their divisiveness, image consciousness, capacity to garner attention and aptness to caricature. They act in this chapter like controls, subjects against which the various modes of televisual caricature can be analysed. The case study is separated into four parts, each of which explores a specific iteration of televisual caricature. 'Scribble' refers to television animation, the most obvious televisual parallel to portrait caricature. Whereas *Margaret Thatcher: Where Am I Now?* (Channel 4, 1999) adapts the cartooning of Steve Bell into short-form animation, *Our Cartoon President* (Showtime, 2018–20) transforms televisual caricature into an animated sitcom. 'Skit' refers to the use of caricature impersonations as part of television sketch shows, analysing a performance of Thatcher in *Psychobitches* (Sky Arts, 2013–14) and Alec Baldwin's famous take on Trump on *Saturday Night Live* (NBC, 1975–). 'Snippet' explores the phenomenon of caricature impersonators appearing in unpredictable ways within television flow, especially as 'guests' on magazine or news programming, considering how such performances work in relation to television's segmental form. Finally, 'Snatch' analyses the coming together of Thatcher and Trump impersonations in *RuPaul's Drag Race UK* (BBC Three, 2019–), examining these performances as examples of 'queer caricature'. These case studies aim to demonstrate the various, often unexpected ways in which caricature appears on television, and how televisual caricature adopts or adapts the methods television uses to address its audience.

The address of televisual caricature

Television's address to viewers, its methods for constructing a viewing public, are a core part of its specificity as a medium. With relatively little literature that specifically assesses how televisual address works, it is a concept that is hidden in plain sight in television scholarship: everywhere alluded to, rarely elucidated. 'Address' is not, for example, one of the 'key concepts' in Casey et al.'s (2008) valuable guide to core ideas in television studies. In introductory textbooks such as *An Introduction to Television Studies* (Bignell, 2013), *Television Studies* (Gray and Lotz, 2019) or *Interpreting Television* (Lury, 2005) and in seminal edited collections on television like *Channels of Discourse* (Allen, 1992b), *The Television Studies Book* (Geraghty and Lusted, 1997) and *The Television Studies Reader* (Allen and Hill, 2004), 'address' does not occupy a space in the index or glossaries of key terms. Notable analyses of televisual address include Michele Hilmes's (1985) exploration of direct address, which applies apparatus theory drawn from film studies to broadcast television; John Ellis's (1992) discussion of direct address as a core component of broadcast television's distinctive use image and sound; Robert C. Allen's (1992a) audience-oriented approach and John Corner's (1995) critical examination of television address as a mode of public communication. The age of this work is striking. It belongs to an earlier generation of television studies of the 1980s and 1990s that emphasises the medium specificity of television as a broadcast form. There has been little updating of work on televisual address, such that the modes of address of twenty-first-century television, a medium with significantly changed industrial, technological, aesthetic and narrative structures, go broadly unremarked upon.

What might hinder the analysis of address? To speak of 'a' televisual address risks simplifying a varied and complex medium, one whose very heterogeneity is crucial. The term appears to collapse the generic, formal and stylistic distinctiveness and diversity of television programming into a set of unlikely universal principles. An analysis of address also appears to privilege the text and its creators as interpellators, and as the locus of meaning. While ideological critique of television on these grounds (often applying Marxist/Structuralist theory and methods) was common in the 1970s, it has gone out of fashion. Successive generations of scholars in cultural, audience and fan studies have rightly challenged this top-down power dynamic and emphasised the active role of the viewer in interpreting televisual communication. Yet, to understand how television functions, what makes it unique as a communication and cultural medium, how it conveys meaning and affect, to come to terms with matters of form, tone, intention, ideology and industry: these are tied up in an understanding of how it addresses an audience, how televisual discourse is framed.

The study of caricature and related discipline, cartooning, offers two main theses on address that are relevant to a study of televisual caricature. The first is to explain how cartoon and caricature address a perceiver anticipated to adopt a viewing position not of the contemplative 'gaze' associated with the normative viewer of art, but instead a 'glancer' or 'skimmer', to borrow the terminology of Raymond N. Morris. Morris notes the insufficiency of 'reader' or 'viewer' to convey a person who is addressed in the expectation that they should get the point of a cartoon in an 'almost instantaneous' manner (1995, 4). This mode of address relates to the context of the encounter that most viewers will have with cartoons: as a visual image that is embedded within the varied offerings of newspapers, journals or magazines. To compete with the other, potentially distracting, stimuli it appears alongside, a cartoon must be visually striking and immediately comprehensible. Though caricatures appear in a range of contexts beyond print, they share with cartoons the need to convey their subjects in a 'condensed or synecdochical form' (Streicher, 1967, 434). The distinction between the gaze and glance mode of viewing is familiar in television studies thanks largely to the influential work of John Ellis, whose *Visible Fictions* (1992) established these as the dominant distinction between the modes of viewing for cinema and TV. Ellis theorises that the viewer of film, because of its intended viewing context (a darkened auditorium, collective engagement, large projected image), is positioned by the cinematic apparatus as adopting a 'gaze' that aids narrative absorption, identification and the operations of visual pleasure. By contrast, television's place as a domestic appliance competing with the many other claims on our attention thrown up by everyday life means that its viewer is assumed to watch in a state of distraction, giving it only the occasional 'glance'. This has obvious implications for how these mediums address their audience. In the case of television, Ellis suggests that it necessitates a constant 'heralding' of the audience back to the set (with an emphasis on sound) as well as images assumed to contain less semiotic complexity than would typically be found in cinema. These understandings of television address have undergone considerable revision to account for changes brought about by industrial transformations, especially the move towards a 'post-network' or 'on-demand' TV culture. Analysis of the address of televisual caricature should then consider its place both within and outside of television flow.

The address to a 'glancing' audience has consequences for the process of distorted recognition, of the (almost) immediate and simultaneous recognition of the caricature subject, the image's unreality, and comic register for the performance (see Introduction). An important distinction here is between two typical modes of address on television, the 'representational' and 'presentational'. When television adopts a representational 'cinematic' mode of address, it 'engages its viewers covertly, making them unseen observers of a world that always appears fully formed and autonomous' (Allen, 1992a, 117). Televisual caricatures in this mode operate in a closed diegesis and are apprehended in a manner analogous to the patterns of recognition and identification associated with characters in narrative fiction. By contrast, the presentational 'rhetorical' mode of address is customary to television that 'simulates the face-to face encounter' and 'acknowledg[es] both the performer's role as addresser and the viewer's role as addressee' (Allen, 1992a, 118). This is commonly found in non-fiction television, for example, in the direct address of a newsreader, chat show host or quizmaster. Representational televisual caricature demands the conventional suspensions of disbelief associated with the consumption of fiction. For presentational televisual caricature this is a little more complex. The overtly fictional caricature performance clashes with normative signifiers of factuality, for example, television presenters, a studio setting and visual aesthetics associated with non-fiction television. This creates a pattern of interaction that Kerry Ferris and Scott R. Harris (2011) describe as the 'frame sophistication' involved in the encounter between celebrity impersonators and audience. Participants in this exchange engage in a silent fluctuation between a 'theatrical frame', which combines 'sincere imitation' and a suspension of disbelief, and a more self-conscious 'playful improvisation', where performers reference their own 'role-taking'. The result of this is an 'impersonation frame' that 'represents an agreement among participants that playful reminders of the performance's unreality are acceptable' (2011, 58). The audience and impersonator (accompanied by the televisual framework that supports their performance) are equal players in this 'impersonation game'. Various cues are adopted to frame televisual caricature, which together form a 'caricature signature' that is a core part of this game. Visual markers, such as hairstyling, make-up and costume, create the 'look' that aids identification of the caricature subject. Dialogue from both the caricature performer and their interlocutors gives contextual indications of how to interpret this televisual moment. This can be complemented by other stylistic properties, including music, set design, props and editing, working together to convey the impersonation frame.

Because caricature and TV address a 'glancer', they not only need to have immediate visual impact, but also rely heavily on what E.H. Gombrich (2002) calls 'the beholder's share', that is, the knowledge, experience and understanding that enable us to decode an image. Caricature is addressed to an active viewer, with references that assume a shared cultural lexicon between creator and beholder. In this sense they are like cartoons, which Ed Ross argues are 'rhetorical exercises which depend on the audience participating in the argument by utilizing its pre-existing knowledge' (2006, 303). The beholder's share relates not only to the viewer's application of their cultural knowledge to the act of interpretation, but also to their disposition. Especially when in satirical mode, caricature addresses viewers as critical and engaged. As Streicher argues, 'the caricature does not aim at "contemplative readers" but at passionate, stand-taking mass reading publics' (1967, 433). The address of caricature can be understood as a caricaturist's interpretation of and dialogue with this public.

Caricatures require of their viewer analogous interpretive practices to irony, described by Linda Hutcheon as 'the making or inferring of meaning in addition to and different from what is stated, together with an attitude toward both the said and the unsaid' (1994, 11). For Hutcheon, the vexed question of intentionality means that the interpreter of irony is tasked not only with attributing meaning but motive. They are helped along in this effort, however, by 'conflictual textual or contextual evidence or by markers which are socially agreed upon' (1994, 11). Caricature similarly requires its perceiver to recognise (but not necessarily accept) the artists' perspective on its target. It offers cues, such as explanatory text, allegorical symbolism or topical references to frame its target and present its case. Televisual caricature adapts these for the medium: on-screen graphic display, voiceover narration, dialogue or non-verbal signifiers (the 'look' of the performer) can give the requisite clues to aid distorted recognition and tonal cues to indicate the expected disposition taken towards the target.

While caricatures may be read as interpretations of a public mood, it is important not to overstate the extent to which they reflect or create this consciousness, nor to assume that any individual will adopt the subject position that they are addressed in. Colin Seymour-Ure resists the idea that the encounter between cartoon and viewer is one of equals, suggesting that the balance of power rests with the viewer. For Seymour-Ure, cartoonists have 'very little control over how it will be understood' because 'appreciation is paradoxically private … it depends heavily on the reader's imagination' (2003, 231). Similarly, Anshuman Mondal (2018) reminds us that, since the emergence of 'mass' (globalised) publics, satiric practice has neither a clearly defined audience nor agreed upon interpretive frameworks for its reception. This means that 'whatever control previous generations of satirists might have had over the ways in which their performances might be interpreted are now no longer available' (2018, 38). The audience 'uptake' of satirical intent cannot be assumed (Caron, 2021, 189–207). The intended address of caricature can fail.

The concept of an address to a viewer using a shared set of coded knowledges is familiar in television studies, thanks to the pioneering work of the Birmingham Centre for Cultural Studies in the 1970s. Stuart Hall's (2007) model of encoding/decoding explains the ideological positioning of television messaging, which is 'encoded' by producers to convey 'preferred meanings'. The interpretive act of 'decoding' happens in the encounter between television discourse and viewers, who draw on their own meaning structures to make sense of these messages. Hall theorises potential viewer responses: dominant/hegemonic, in which the receiver accepts the message as it was encoded; oppositional, the rejection of the encoded meaning and reading of it according to an alternative framework; and negotiated, a reading strategy that mediates between oppositional and hegemonic based on the subject position of the decoder. Televisual caricature's critical mode of address complicates the process of encoding and decoding. Caricature has occupied contradictory historical positions, as both oppositional or anti-elitist, *and* hegemonic, implicated in maintaining exclusions and oppressions (Herhuth, 2018). The 'preferred meaning' of televisual caricature is frequently one that is, at least superficially, counter-hegemonic or sceptical of dominant ideologies and those who promote them.

In both TV and caricature there exists a tension between the intimate address to private individuals, and the communal viewing practice that renders its discourse public. For this reason, TV has been seen, since the mid-twentieth century, as a critical medium of the democratic public sphere. Jürgen Habermas's (1992) concept of the (bourgeois) public sphere, an arena in which citizens engage in the rational discourse necessary for a functioning democracy, was taken up by political economists and social theorists in the defence of public service broadcasting (Curran, 1991; Garnham, 1992; Dahlgren, 1995). Television's role in the public sphere is conceived largely as an informational one, associated with non-fiction genres of news, current affairs and (some) documentary, assumed to provide members of the public with the tools needed to participate in citizenship. Rebecca Wanzo posits caricature as a 'citizenship genre', that is, 'categories of representation that the state's subjects are interpellated to inhabit' (2020, 3). For Wanzo, caricature implicitly indicates who should be included in the category of 'citizenship' and has therefore been an 'indelible part of how citizenship discourses have circulated' (2020, 6). Wanzo's study of African American caricature highlights the negative role the form has played in racist exclusions from citizenship, a necessary reminder that while caricatures may act as a public critique that uses ridicule to limit an individual's power, they also have a long history of perpetuating cultural and political marginalisation or oppression (see Chapter 4).

Exclusions like these from the public sphere have been central to critiques of the concept. Nancy Fraser (1992), for example, drew attention to the existence of 'subaltern counterpublics', groups marginalised in the public sphere who nevertheless find alternative means of expression for their identities. These are often treated as cultural rather than political, associated with the private sphere and kept separate from analyses of the public sphere. Scholars such as Jim McGuigan (2005, 2011) and John Hartley (Hartley and Green, 2006; Hartley, 2010) have posited the concept of the 'cultural public sphere' to account for the importance of affect as well as reason in the practice and experience of citizenship. The concept reclaims for the public sphere the 'aesthetic and emotional engagement with lifeworld issues' associated with fiction genres (McGuigan, 2011, 83). The cultural public sphere, for Hartley and Green, 'represent[s] an interzone between culture and politics' that can 'express values and identities that are not found generally in the public sphere of rational debate about the real' (2006, 349). Hartley later argued that the active use of popular media (including television) has enabled people excluded from 'classic citizenship' to engage instead in 'media citizenship', which he argues is 'bottom up, self-organising, voluntarist, tolerant of diversity and also a good deal more fun for participants than the modernist minimalism of the Habermasian public sphere' (2010, 239). Crucially, the concept of media citizenship includes entertainment and comedy as well as informational genres. For McGuigan, fiction enjoys a greater licence to 'articulat[e] politics … as a contested terrain' (2011, 83) than news programming, where representation is more closely policed, both formally through regulation and politically through censorious discourse. McGuigan identifies satirical comedy as an example of a cultural form in which political ideas that are marginalised in mainstream communication can be aired. Hartley similarly notes that political comedy has become a 'go-to source for civic understanding', a practice he describes as 'silly citizenship', in which 'both professional and amateur creativity [are] expended in the cause of political agency' (2010, 241). James E. Caron (2021) sees television satire as an essential expression of the 'comic public sphere', a parodic supplement to the public sphere that promotes its values of reasoned debate, accountability and facticity, though modified for an era in which faith in them has been eroded. Televisual caricature has potential value as a means of expressing concepts that are restricted more broadly in televisual discourse, whether that is because they are regulated out or are politically inexpedient for broadcasters. While it is sometimes celebrated for the quasi-informational role of informing the public about a political class and its key figures, television has a broader value in the encouragement of 'silly citizenship', engagement with the cultural or comic public sphere.

Edward Lucie-Smith argues that caricature is a 'popular and public' form; by virtue of the rapidity and cheapness of the print medium, it is a mode of communication that 'speaks to us privately, as individuals' yet is 'available to almost anyone' (1981, 13). The parallel with broadcast television here is obvious. Both modes make a virtue of the immediacy, ephemerality and demotic quality of their medium to communicate ideas about the world to their publics. However, TV's supposed address to mass audiences has undergone significant transformation in its journey from a broadcast to an on-demand medium. This is commonly periodised as the transition between TVI, the era of analogue broadcast television as a mass medium; TVII, multichannel broadcast which fragmented audiences and compelled demographic targeting and narrowcasting; TVIII, dominated by time-shift technologies that moved television into a commodity rather than service form; and TVIV, the era of subscription video on demand (SVOD) and a proliferation of content (Jenner, 2016). The development of television in this way has necessitated a sharpening of address to audiences that are increasingly specified by markers of identity, such as age, gender, sexuality, class, level of education, special interests or political affiliation. The consequences of this, including the creation of politically polarised informational 'filter bubbles' and a 'post-broadcast democracy', are well known (Prior, 2007). These changes have also had a clear impact on the address (and the industrial positioning – see Chapter 3) of televisual caricature. Analysing televisual caricature's framing of its subject means paying attention to the contextual and paratextual cues (such as channel or provider, schedule position or catalogue entry on on-demand platforms) that suggest who is its presumed or ideal addressee. It is also important to be mindful of caricature's tendency towards confirmation bias, to reaffirm the pre-existing knowledges and dispositions of its perceiver (Herhuth, 2018).

Modes of address in both television and caricature provide a framework for interpretation, to indicate quickly and efficiently to the viewer both how to interpret the image and the disposition to take towards it. As Ross notes, 'the power of framing is not power to specify what to think of a situation, but instead power to suggest how to think of a situation' (2006, 285). What is required, then, to frame a caricature using televisual address? First, a televisual caricature must communicate immediately the identity of its target, using some combination of strong visual cues in the facial and bodily image (e.g. hairstyle, costume, make-up) that emphasise the 'caricature signature'; aural markers in dialogue or voiceover communication, but also in the vocal impression; graphic overlay before or during the caricature performance; and performative cues from non-caricature performers. Each of these signals communicates the identity of the subject and enables recognition that it is a caricature. Second, TV caricature must indicate, via tone and mode of address, the disposition the viewer is anticipated to adopt towards the subject. Presented in humorous mode, the televisual caricature will usually be proposed as a light iteration of representation, an unserious but not necessarily trivial reproduction of a famous persona. It will (usually) exaggerate and lampoon its subject in ways that are socially, culturally and institutionally sanctioned at the time of its broadcast and appropriate to the genre and format of the programme in which it appears. This must fit with the prevailing cultural politics of the time, the context of its broadcast or distribution (for example, its place in the schedule) and the institutional ethos of the broadcaster or media organisation which makes and disseminates the content. Third, the caricature must be framed in such a way that its distinction from the regular truth claims of television is clearly apparent. The conventions of television form and image are employed to present the deception that this caricature 'is' the subject, while simultaneously specific cues are adopted to clarify that the impersonation is a fiction. Televisual caricature's power as an artefact of the cultural or comic public sphere depends on the maintenance of the fiction alongside a self-consciousness about its reference to reality. Finally, each of these factors must be sufficient that a viewer can bring to the caricature their own knowledge and interpretive ability, to enable instantaneous recognition. Televisual caricature stretches and destabilises the medium's norms of address, rapidly creating a specific frame of reference in which comic impersonation can be read simultaneously as a representation *and* a distortion of a real public figure that crystallises for the viewer a series of culturally accepted ideas about that subject. To demonstrate how this works in practice, and across a range of programme contexts, I turn my attention now to case studies of two highly recognisable, often repeated, televisual caricatures.

Margaret and Donald: The multiple faces of televisual caricature

Margaret Thatcher and Donald Trump have been repeatedly caricatured, on television and beyond. Both politicians strategically constructed visually striking, powerful public personas, created through a combination of self-mythologisation, media training and self-conscious performance. These political personas are eminently reproducible and imitable, a gift to caricaturists and impersonators. During Thatcher's time in office, televisual impersonations of the prime minister by actors such as Faith Brown, Janet Brown or Maureen Lipman were a regular occurrence, appearing in a range of genres from light entertainment to news broadcast. Marcus Harmes (2013) notes in his study of parodies of Thatcher that her distinctive image and voice made her easy to caricature, and that exaggerations of her features are common in media portrayals. Even before Trump ran for president, it was a cliché to note that he is a cartoonish figure whose utterances, attitude and actions are unsatirisable because they are too extreme. Both figures have been dependent on visual media, particularly television, to construct and proliferate this public persona, creating what Martin Murray (2022) calls a 'synergetic' relationship between politician, public and media.[1] There have been numerous scholarly appraisals of Thatcher and Trump's mediated images and their legacy (Baxter, 1991; Nunn, 2002; Hadley and Ho, 2010; Kellner, 2016; Boczkowski and Papacharissi, 2018; Poniewozik, 2019). Here, I add televisual caricatures to this mix. I demonstrate, via analyses of various iterations of Thatcher/Trump depictions, the range of methods, formats and modes in which televisual caricature can be seen, applying the analysis of caricature form and televisual address to specific examples. These are animated caricature (scribble), caricature as part of sketch comedy (skit), caricature as an unpredictable part of television flow (snippet) and caricature performance as part of a reality competition show (snatch).

Scribble

Animation, bringing drawing to life, represents the closest moving image equivalent to traditional caricature; indeed, according to Eric Herhuth, 'caricatures want to be animated to fulfil their imminent transformation: to become a single coherent figure' (2018, 642). Animated caricature appears in various TV forms, such as children's television, advertising or interstitials. It is not unusual for famous figures to be caricatured for one-off appearances in animated sitcoms, such as *The Simpsons* (Fox, 1989–), *South Park* (Comedy Central, 1997–) or *BoJack Horseman* (Netflix, 2014–20). A memorable example is George Bush Sr in *The Simpsons* ('Two Bad Neighbors', Season 7, Episode 13), in an

---

[1] Murray is describing Trump here, but the idea is applicable to other powerful political media figures.

episode in which the former president moves near the Simpson family. Bush publicly criticised the show, promising to make Americans 'more like the Waltons, and less like the Simpsons', and his appearance in this episode clearly has satirical intent. There is also considerable pleasure to be had in seeing a well-known face re-rendered in *The Simpsons*' distinctive animated style, in the 'distorted recognition' of a famous politician. The design of the Bush caricature includes thin, pursed lips in a permanent scowl, implying his joyless pedanticism, and an extension of Bush's large forehead, both a somewhat unkind ridiculing of his receding hairline and a metaphorical reminder of his elitism, a literal high-brow. Celebrity 'cameos' in long-running series do not necessarily present a satirical critique of their subject but do draw on the caricature practice of humorous exaggeration of the persona and image.

Our Cartoon President expands this tendency in animated sitcom by composing its entire primary cast of characters from members of the Trump family, prominent Republican and Democrat politicians, and political journalists like Anderson Cooper, Rachel Maddow or the hosts of *Fox and Friends* (Fox News, 1998–). The show started life as a recurring feature on *The Late Show With Stephen Colbert* (CBS, 2015–26), and was marketed on the strength of Colbert's personal association with political satire. Unlike *The Late Show*, which, thanks to its production style and daily scheduling, can include up-to-date humour on recent political developments, *Our Cartoon President* is not truly topical. As Rafał Kuś (2022) notes, the restrictions of animated sitcom format impede the series from being entirely up to date, exacerbated by the sheer pace of political change and regularity of controversy during the first Trump administration. *Our Cartoon President*'s production team aimed for a middle approach of pre-written scripted episodes with short audio inserts with topical humour dubbed into the episodes during postproduction. Kuś argues that this makes the programme feel more like a traditional sitcom than a political satire, combining the traditions of the family and workplace sitcom. In the caricature of Trump, two comedic types combine: the inadequate patriarch and the incompetent boss. The specifics of Trump's own personality (that is, how his personality is interpreted by the programme-makers), his narcissism, callousness, short attention span, greed and childishness, are overlaid on these broader tropes to translate the president into an animated sitcom caricature.

The series regularly incorporates video footage of the real Trump (as well as other characters), providing an immediate point of comparison between cartoon diegesis and reality, and, by extension, a useful contextual and tonal cue for interpretation. This aids not only in the pleasure of distorted recognition, but also playfully implies a continuity between the caricature iteration of the Trumps and their real personas. In the first episode, 'State of the Union', the animated caricatures watch and recognise themselves in the (fictionalised) television documentary *An American Family*, creating the liminal space between reality and fiction typical of satire. This faux-documentary airs on the Fox Network, which features in *Our Cartoon President* as 'Trump's' favourite media outlet, as well as parodying its sycophantic news anchors. While liberal news programming (CNN and MSNBC) is also ridiculed, the Fox Network is presented as a dangerous cult that brainwashes its audience. This implies that there is little anticipated alignment between the viewers of Fox News and of *Our Cartoon President*, the latter implicitly addressed as having the media literacy to avoid such indoctrination. The originating network for *Our Cartoon President*, Showtime, is a premium entertainment cable channel which is well known for making provocative, 'quality' television for an upmarket audience. The distaste shown by *Our Cartoon President* for Trump, his supporters and his favoured media outlets fits with broader tribal demographics in US entertainment media and politics. Through its references to, and burlesques on, the real speeches, actions and attitudes of Trump, it addresses a viewer knowledgeable about and, implicitly, opposed to the real figure.

Our Cartoon President's design for Trump replicates the 'tabs of identity' (Seymour-Ure, 2003, 244) that form his caricature signature: gravity-defying blond hairstyle, orange-tinged tan, whitened eyelids, jowls, ill-fitting suit with elongated red tie and small hands. The series comically responds to the easy replicability of these features in its second episode, 'Disaster Response', in which 'Trump' hires a series of impersonators to replace him for presidential responsibilities in which he is not interested. The idea of doing so occurs to 'Trump' when he is late-night channel surfing and encounters a different comedic impersonator on each channel, a shrewd recognition of the ubiquity of Trump televisual caricature during his presidency. 'Trump' is flattered rather than offended, a joke at the expense of his narcissism, but also an acknowledgement of the ego massage caricatures can offer their subjects. He puts the impersonators through a Trump 'boot camp', training them in gluttony, insult-throwing, oratorial incoherence and responsibility evasion. They are dressed and made up to closely resemble Trump, highlighting the artificiality and imitability of his image and persona (Fig. 2.1). In 'Disaster Response', *Our Cartoon President* deconstructs the role of televisual caricature, highlighting the features of comedic impersonation, and noting that, for a public figure like Trump, their satirical project may be counterproductive. Rather than weakening 'Trump', the

Fig. 2.1 Donald Trump trains a legion of impersonators to replace him for everyday tasks, *Our Cartoon President*

impersonators lend him a clear strategic advantage, by amplifying and affirming the success of the self-constructed persona.

Where *Our Cartoon President* represents an intra-medial translation of a television segment into a sitcom format, *Margaret Thatcher: Where Am I Now?* offers an example of the intermedial adaptation of a newspaper caricature to TV animation. This was a series of five-minute shorts, broadcast immediately after the *Channel 4 News* in April 1999, which adapted the work of cartoonist Steve Bell, best known for a daily cartoon 'If …' in *The Guardian* (1981–2021). The series parodies a political memoir and is posed as a personal account of twentieth-century history and a haughty self-assessment delivered by 'Thatcher' as she contemplates herself in a mirror. The mirror is returned to throughout the series as a shorthand signifier for self-reflection but also to remind the viewer of the self-consciousness with which the Thatcher persona was created. This is evident from the first episode, which opens with a grotesque sequence in which Thatcher is portrayed as a rusting automaton, her face refurbished using tools such as screwdrivers that cause her eyes to turn in their sockets (a reference to Thatcher's faintly lazy eye that is regularly exaggerated by caricaturists) or a blowtorch that turns her skin a dotted metallic blue (Fig. 2.2). The emphasis from the beginning is on the construction of a public image, which includes the voiceover narration that tells Thatcher's story in a self-serving, first-person narrative. The narration is delivered by actress Sally Grace in an impression that heightens Thatcher's sonorous tone, clipped accent and slow pace of delivery to match the grandiosity of the storytelling. The voiceover lampoons Thatcher's pompous oratorial style, especially her fondness for biblical quotation; Episode Four, for example, parodies her use of religious rhetoric to justify her economic policies: 'for unto everyone that hath shall be given, and he shall have abundance; but from him that hath not shall be taken away even that which he hath; and cast ye the unprofitable servant into darkness'. The series satirises Thatcher's parochialism and religiosity via its main soundtrack theme, a pastiche of English patriotic and hymnal music played on an

Fig. 2.2 Margaret Thatcher presented as a rusting automaton, *Margaret Thatcher: Where Am I Now?*

electronic organ. The combination of these elements produces a surreal, queasily nostalgic tone for the series.

Each episode begins with a title card, a still image of a straitjacketed Thatcher being escorted from Downing Street by police. The implication is that what follows are the reflections of an unstable mind, and so we should view her as an unreliable narrator. This is continued throughout the series in the contrast between the views espoused by the caricature with archive footage. This acts not only as an *aide memoire* for the events referred to, but also to create ironic juxtapositions between 'Thatcher's' interpretation, as delivered in the voiceover, and visible reality. For example, Episode Four opens with 'Thatcher's' voiceover boasting of the success of her economic policies, while the image consists of a montage of building demolitions, an obvious visual indictment of the destructiveness of her government's agenda. She continues by claiming a 'new public mood was evident, given joyful expression in the celebration surrounding the wedding of the Prince of Wales and Lady Diana Spencer'. This is illustrated by images of violent clashes between police and protesters, followed by a caricature of Charles and Diana being hit with a bottle thrown from off screen. This continuity between the actuality footage and the animation serves to highlight the distortions of these events in 'Thatcher's' presentation of them. *Where Am I Now?* delivers not only a visual caricature of Thatcher, but, in its spoof of her autobiography, it satirises her attitudes and political perspective. The 'preferred reading' encoded in the caricature is an ironic one that invites the viewer to adopt a position sceptical of, even oppositional to, 'Thatcher's' version of events.

The programme was broadcast to mark twenty years since the General Election campaign of 1979 which ushered Thatcher into power, an anniversary that prompted a broader cultural reflection on her influence on the UK's political environment in the late 1990s (McElwee, 1999; *The Guardian*, 1999). Two themes were prominent in these reappraisals: first, to highlight Thatcher's success, since her economic policies had been broadly adopted by British politicians as the new ideological baseline; and second, that then prime minister Tony Blair had embraced her charisma-driven, presidential style of governance and was therefore her political heir despite leading the Labour Party (Nunn, 2002). *Where Am I Now?* adopts this critical position. In the first episode, the voiceover narration discusses the state of the nation at the end of 'this turbulent millennium', one that is 'proud, strong, confident and free, certain of its position at the centre of the world stage, ... and cast in my own image'. Blair, and his wife, Cherie, are depicted as caricatures, wide-eyed and with glistening smiles, waving to an off-screen public. A zoom in to 'Blair's' eye dissolves and zooms out to reveal 'Thatcher's' mirror image. This implies a direct line of continuity between Thatcher and Blair. A similar visual match edit of a closeup of their eyes suggests the same of the leader of the Conservatives, William Hague, who is pictured as a schoolboy reaching for 'Thatcher's' hand before she uses it to smack his head. Imagery like this, which implies a maternal link between Thatcher and politicians of the 1990s, is consistent with the tendency in British cartooning of the late twentieth century to use these 'parodic reiterations' of Thatcher to metonymically represent the continued prevalence of Thatcherite ideology across the political spectrum (Joyce, 2010). Television editing's ability to construct an implied causal link between these images sharpens the critique. Heather Joyce argues that 'depictions of Blair repeating or parodying Thatcher threaten to resituate Thatcher as a locus of political and cultural nostalgia' (2010, 239). *Where Am I Now?* subverts this nostalgia through televisual caricature. It is a fictionalisation that invites its viewer to reflect critically on other retellings of the Thatcher story. In this sense, it acted as an addition from the 'cultural public sphere' to the broader public analysis of Thatcher's legacy taking place across various media in May 1999.

As well as bearing in mind the political context for *Where Am I Now*'s broadcast, it is also instructive to consider Channel 4's industrial position at the time of transmission. The 1990s was a transitional period for the broadcaster. During the 1980s, it developed an institutional culture of risk-taking, broadcasting programmes that addressed a range of minority interests thanks to a funding formula that did not require it to deliver mass audiences to advertisers, and a legislated remit to innovate and experiment. The Broadcasting Act of 1990 required Channel 4 to sell its own advertising airtime after 1993. To avoid direct competition with popular commercial rival ITV, it began strategically to target demographics sought after by advertisers, including educated professionals (ABC1 consumers) assumed to have high levels of disposable income, and hard-to-reach 'light' television viewers (Brown, 2007). Channel 4's political programming, especially its news bulletin, addressed audiences as well-informed and critical, presenting itself as an alternative voice on British television. *Where Am I Now?* was broadcast at 7.55 p.m., between the end of the *Channel 4 News* and the beginning of the evening schedule, a slot typically occupied on the channel by informational, political or experimental shorts. It aligns with the tone and aims of Channel 4's branding at this time. It offers not only an oppositional caricature of Thatcher (one translated from another left-liberal brand in *The Guardian*), but also an implicit critique of the continuation of Thatcherism in New Labour. Political comedy was broadcast regularly on Channel 4 in the 1990s, offering a light counterpoint to mainstream political discourse typical of the 'comic public sphere' (Caron, 2021). Particularly prominent was Rory Bremner, whose impersonations of politicians, Blair especially, were a regular fixture on Channel 4 in *Rory Bremner, Who Else* (1993–8) and *Bremner, Bird and Fortune* (1999–2010). Bremner's Blair caricature appears in the interstitial material immediately following some broadcasts of *Where Am I Now?* (for example, Episode Two), in a trailer for 'Channel 4's Political Weekend' (1–2 May 1999), offering in-character humorous remarks about the programming. It concludes with 'Channel 4. Good, isn't it? Anyone want to buy it?', referencing the Blair government's continuation of Thatcher's privatisation agenda. Interstitial material thus folds the Thatcher caricature into Channel 4's political comedy branding, framing its address to a savvy, knowing viewer.

Both *Our Cartoon President* and *Where Am I Now?* exploit animation's medial affordances to reproduce their subjects as grotesque and fantastical. In their shared combination of animation with archive footage, they remind the viewer of the caricature's position between fiction and reality. The animated caricature displays the constructed political persona. The juxtaposition between real image and animated caricature critiques the subject, implying that they are as much artificial creations as each other. Both programmes appeared on networks that, at their time of broadcast, were targeting a specific audience of politically engaged liberals. These animated caricatures share an ironic tone that assumes a viewer that is knowing, media literate and politically opposed to their subjects. Animation's visual difference from most television material lends it a distinctiveness that immediately conveys to a 'glancer' its caricature quality. But not all televisual caricature is animated. How then, can performed caricature, in which the impersonator fully embodies the target, be framed using televisual language?

Skit

Sketch shows built around comic impersonation have been a recurring feature on UK television since the 1970s. These can be ensemble efforts such as *Who Do You Do?* (LWT, 1972–6), *Dead Ringers* (BBC Two, 2002–7) and *The Impressions Show* (BBC One, 2009–11) or star vehicles designed to display the skill of impressionists such as Mike Yarwood, Faith Brown, Alistair McGowan and Morgana Robinson. Sketch comedy is made up of a series of short, loosely connected skits, which requires it to communicate its comic ideas rapidly, often using caricature practices such as simplification and exaggeration to achieve this. Impersonations of real people within skits combine caricature with the structural and stylistic elements of sketch comedy: short-form narratives; expository dialogue that rapidly sets the scene and provides a set up for punchlines; heightened, often parodic, performance styles; and costume, hair and make-up designed for immediate visual impact. These generic elements, alongside paratextual signals (scheduling, title sequences, listings, reviews and so on) construct a hermeneutic frame for viewers, setting expectations about the kinds of representation they will encounter. Conventionally, these programmes adopt a representational mode, translating the televisual caricature subject into a sketch character and building jokes around the exaggeration and, sometimes, subversion of the subject's persona. Televisual caricature is a natural fit for a programme format that presents humorous, exaggerated, simplified characters as part of its generic functioning.

Psychobitches is a sketch comedy programme broadcast by narrowcast channel Sky Arts in the early 2010s. Its central conceit is that a series of famous historical or mythical women are undergoing treatment by a present-day psychiatrist (Rebecca Front), with comically surreal results. Margaret Thatcher (Michelle Gomez) appears as the subject of two skits in the first episode of Series 2. The first satirises Thatcher via an intertextual alignment with Hannibal Lecter, specifically the depiction by Anthony Hopkins in *The Silence of the Lambs* (Jonathan Demme, 1991). It begins without revealing its subject; rather we see an anonymous figure wearing a straitjacket and full-face mask, wheeled on a vertical trolley through a dimly lit corridor (Fig. 2.3). The next shot, a low-angled medium close-up, reveals a royal blue skirt and sensible black high-heeled pumps; costuming that is a core part of the Thatcher caricature signature. Thatcher is confirmed as the skit's target when the mask is removed to reveal the face, with a red-lipsticked mouth over which a sinister, cool smile plays, and hair, strawberry blonde, set, backcombed and teased into a large bouffant. Allegorical uses of cultural references within caricature have been common throughout its history, especially figures from mythology and folklore (Lucie-Smith, 1981; Feaver, 1981). Citing Hopkins's Lecter as a signifier of lunacy, psychopathy and monstrosity allows the caricature to accuse Thatcher of these flaws by proxy. The straitjacket as a signifier of madness is similarly invoked in the opening titles of *Where Am I Now?* and both caricatures adopt it as shorthand to dispute the rationality of Thatcher's political philosophies. The caricature addresses an intended audience that concurs with this assessment or at least will find pleasure in the ironic parallels between Thatcher and Lecter. For the Thatcher detractor these are not incongruous juxtapositions but

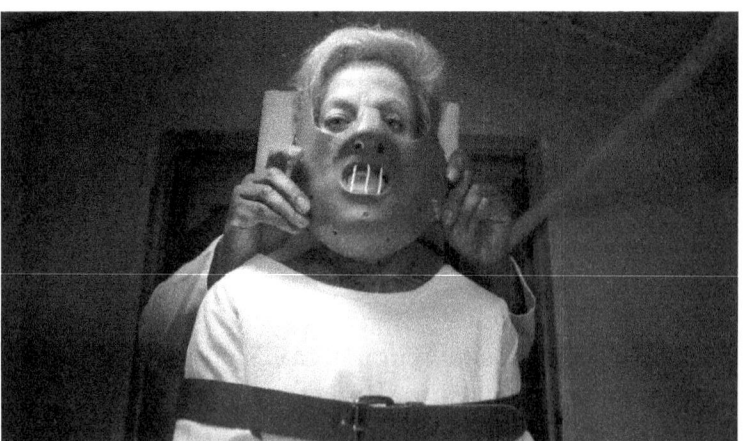

Fig. 2.3 Margaret Thatcher (Michelle Gomez) caricatured via Hannibal Lecter in *Psychobitches*

apt comparisons, performing the caricature's role of externalising inner flaws.

Much of *Psychobitches*' humour comes from using the therapy milieu to subvert expectations about famous historical figures, offering either an incongruous alternative view of their inner life by comparison to the well-known aspects of their public persona, or by absurdly exaggerating that persona. The second Thatcher skit adopts the latter approach. In *Psychobitches*, the therapist acts as the 'straight woman' to the caricatures, the conscience of the programme that presents a reasoned perspective and expected behavioural norms against which the caricature's eccentricities can be measured (Andrews, 2019). In the second skit, she asks 'Thatcher' if there are dangers in viewing the world as she does. 'Thatcher' responds by denying that she has a 'view of the world', claiming merely to see the things as they are. This statement, given the context in which it is being aired and the manner of its delivery, is presented as inherently absurd. Michelle Gomez provides an accurate vocal impression of Thatcher's careful delivery, low pitch, arhythmical cadence and soft consonant sounds. She mimics Thatcher's posture, the stiffness and stillness of her shoulders, her tendency to tilt her head and direct her gaze, contorting her face to replicate the widened eyes and intense gaze that are prominent in many Thatcher caricatures (especially, as we have seen, in Steve Bell's work). Gomez combines the Thatcher caricature signature with the actor's unpredictable, faintly menacing style of delivery, visible in her performance as other caricatures on *Psychobitches*, on sitcom *Green Wing* (Channel 4, 2004–7) or as a villain on *Doctor Who* (BBC, 1964–). 'Thatcher' continues by railing against the 'socialist' view that we are all made equal, in her view a 'disgusting perversion of the truth'. As she delivers her disputation of the idea that 'we all have innate value', she cannot finish the final word and vomits profusely in disgust. The sketch employs caricature grotesquery to critique not only Thatcher's persona, but the belief system that she embodies. This violent rejection of a seemingly inoffensive, blandly liberal philosophy is humorous only if we assume a viewer who does not share Thatcher's ideological positioning or is able to maintain a comic distance from their own political orientation and make a negotiated reading of the skit. The sketch encodes a preferred reading that adopts the position presented by the psychiatrist, who acts as the rational voice in the exchange and an avatar for the viewer.

Much as *Psychobitches*' Thatcher caricature addresses a viewer with a sceptical or oppositional view of its target, so too does Alec Baldwin's infamous *Saturday Night Live* (*SNL*) impersonation of Donald Trump. This follows an established pattern for *SNL* of creating caricatures of prominent political figures by making them into recurring sketch characters, typically as part of the 'cold open' segment that appears before the show's first commercial break and title sequence (Jones, 2013). During the 2016 election cycle, *SNL* skits parodied televised debates between Trump and Hillary Clinton (Kate McKinnon) in episodes broadcast on 1, 15 and 22 October. Costuming and styling for the actors closely reproduces those of their caricature targets in the debates, providing a frame of reference against which the skit should be compared. The set design replicates the studio stages in which the real debates took place, and the editing pattern reproduces the conventional pattern for televising them: a multi-camera combination of medium shots of the individual speaker (sometimes in split screen to capture the reactions of both candidates) with a wide shot showing both podia. This creates a familiar backdrop against which the 'impersonation game', with its oscillation between reality and fiction, takes place (Ferris and Harris, 2011). Baldwin copies Trump's signature actions and speech patterns: the finger-pinching hand gesture, the animated face, the pursed mouth, the mispronunciation of the word 'China' (as 'jina'). Much of the humour derives from the exaggeration of these signatures through repetition, amplification of the vocal impression or greater animation of the body. Baldwin's impersonation makes overt what is usually implicit in Trump's actions or speech, such as his obvious attempts to suppress his anger or aggression to appear 'presidential'. In doing so, it performs caricature's theorised function of externalising inner flaws, even if such externalisation requires only the slightest nudge from beneath the surface.

SNL's Trump caricature presents a tension between representational and presentational style. Some skits are representational, using the caricature as a character in a sitcom-style scene, such as preparing for the presidency with his advisers (broadcast 19 November 2016), or interacting with other world leaders in the cafeteria at a NATO summit (broadcast 7 December 2019). Most are parodies of presentational televisual programming, where TV's rhetorical mode of address is used to communicate with the public, such as debates, addresses and press conferences. The viewer is invited to move between suspension of disbelief in this comic simulation and their memory of the real mediations of Trump that are being evoked. These skits make self-conscious jokes about this traversal of the reality/unreality boundary. For example, the cold open for the show that aired on 14 January 2017 presents itself in onscreen graphic and voiceover as a 'rebroadcast' of Trump's first press conference as president elect, which had taken place three days before (see Fig. 2.4). Baldwin's Trump opens with 'I just want to address the question that's on everyone's mind: yes this is real life, this is really happening'. This is a metacommentary on the extreme unpredictability of US politics at the time of the broadcast, assuming an ideal viewer who was not expecting Trump's victory and encoding a preferred reading

Fig. 2.4 Donald Trump (Alec Baldwin) directly addresses the American public in a parody of a presidential speech, *Saturday Night Live*

from a liberal subject position. It addresses an audience who have difficulty believing it is, and perhaps wish this was not, real life.

Christopher J. Gilbert (2021) argues that Baldwin's Trump follows in the tradition of satirical caricature in working to reveal 'true' character, borrowing from the form's rhetorical force to offer a 'character assassination' of the president. Amy B. Becker (2020) similarly notes the scathing tone and evident bias of the caricature, comparing it to a political attack advert. Her audience research suggests that the Baldwin caricature renders Trump more 'human', prone to mistakes because he is a 'celebrity first, not a politician', hence viewers compare the real Trump positively with the caricature (2021, 156). Beyond merely traducing Trump's character, Baldwin's caricature creates the paradoxical effect of benefitting the target by reiterating and amplifying his carefully curated media persona. According to Will Howell and Trevor Parry-Giles the caricature represents a 'new rhetorical role for presidential impersonations in an era of polarized politics' (2018, 152). Prior to Baldwin's Trump, they argue, such impersonations provided a 'simulation' of the president, one that manifests some of the characteristics of presidential performance rather than simply a pretence, such that 'the impersonation's meaning … lies in the circumscribed gap between "reality" and the believable, plausible simulation' (2018, 152). Caricature's humanisation of the president is useful, they argue, as means to resolve the tension between the ideal figureheads of the public imagination and the real, flawed individuals who assume the office. In this sense they perform a valuable service as part of the 'comic public sphere', both prompting sober reflection on the necessary requirements for political leadership and an acceptance of the reality that the office is held by a human being. For Howell and Parry-Giles, Baldwin's Trump represents a departure from this model, designed not for this conciliatory purpose, but to galvanise the president's opponents into political action. Because Baldwin's approximation of Trump is so close to the reality of his target's persona, Parry-Giles and Howell conclude that the caricature addresses its audience with the assumption that both the impersonation *and* the real Trump are improper simulations of an American president. Trump's eventual election in 2016 shows that *SNL*'s televisual caricature of Trump was unsuccessful in its aim to use ridicule to highlight his dangerous unsuitability for the office of president. His re-election in 2024 – as well as the noticeable absence of substantial televisual caricatures of Trump during his campaign – suggests something perhaps more disturbing. Political reality appears to have reached a 'new normal', such that a level of irrationality, unpredictability and uncertainty that what was once absurd and caricaturable is now standard, unremarkable and no longer funny. In contrast to Marx's famous maxim, history seems to be repeating itself, first as farce, now as tragedy.

SNL and *Psychobitches* demonstrate how caricatures can be incorporated within the structures of sketch comedy. Through intertextual allusion, or the close approximation of mediated events, these caricatures use references to critique their subject, assuming a viewer with sufficient knowledge to be able to decode them. They also construct humour from their closeness to, rather than incongruity with, the real figure they represent. Both skit caricatures also address a viewer with a moderate, liberal worldview, against which the subject's conservative beliefs are contrasted humorously. Whereas *Psychobitches* directly ridicules Thatcher's right-wing political beliefs, using her metonymically to reflect broader conservative ideology, *SNL* tends to direct its critique at the person rather than party or ideology. It is for this reason that *SNL* caricatures have been described as 'pseudo-satire' (Declercq, 2018) and critiqued for their potential to diffuse rather than encourage critique among citizens and to humanise their target. An alternative reading, along the lines argued by Howell and Parry-Giles, is that Trump marked a such a departure from the norms of presidential conduct that the caricature's revelation of the nature of his persona performed a valuable function in the 'comic public sphere', a means of confronting citizens with the absurdity of political reality rather than rendering politics absurd. These televisual caricatures address a viewer with the wealth of knowledge about and an oppositional disposition towards their subjects, providing a necessary relief from the grim reality that is also evoked in the parody of them.

Snippet

Animation or impersonation-based skits are predictable forms of televisual mediation for caricature, but they are not the only spaces in which televisual caricature appears. It can also be seen in 'snippet' form as part of the flow of more various programming such as advertising, chat shows, magazine programmes, talent competitions and television news broadcasts. Snippet televisual caricatures are difficult to pin down because of their very ephemeral nature. They are intended to be seen but not necessarily to be remembered, to have a momentary rather than a lasting impact. They therefore require a directness that functions well within the segmental structure of broadcast flow, as influentially analysed by John Ellis (1992). The ephemerality of snippet caricatures requires a structure of address to an 'unsuspecting' audience. For an animated sitcom or sketch show, paratextual framing mechanisms such as continuity announcements, title sequences, the presence of a studio audience (in the case of *Saturday Night Live*) or a predictable format work to contain and contextualise the caricature. Snippet caricature does not necessarily have this paratextual support to structure its address to an audience, since it is found in contexts outside of these controlled environments. In snippet caricature, performers usually adopt a presentational pose of embodying their caricatured subject, pretending to be the figure in an improvised (televisual) scenario. In snippet-form caricature, the 'impersonation frame' must be conveyed swiftly and immediately through visual, aural and performance cues that bring the viewer into the joke.

An examination of two instances of snippet caricature will illuminate this further. The first is a short segment from an April 1985 broadcast of TVAM's *Good Morning Britain*, ITV's first breakfast television magazine programme. It begins as host Mike Morris abruptly halts an interview with actor Nigel Hawthorne. Morris holds a hand up to his ear, a familiar gesture in live television to indicate that the presenter is being fed information by a producer in his earpiece. He tells Hawthorne there's 'an important moment happening on our forecourt', and the image shifts from the studio to an Outside Broadcast camera, which captures a car arriving outside the building. A familiar silhouette can be seen in the back of the car, the unmistakeable flash of red-blonde hair, and a blue suit. Morris emphasises the effectiveness of these semiotic cues as he says, 'Nigel, you must recognise the figure in the back', to which Hawthorne audibly assents. For a few seconds, the reality status of these images is in question, the televisual grammar applied so far offers little to indicate this is a hoax. It is only when the figure that emerges from the car is clearly not Thatcher, but a man dressed as her, that it becomes clear that the previous thirty seconds have been the comedic set up for a punchline: a caricature, not the real thing. Laughter among the crew and guests can be heard even as Morris continues his commentary as though this really were Thatcher, his mode of address now shifted to an ironic tone rather than the more straightforward delivery of the previous seconds.

Thatcher is portrayed in this snippet by Steve Nallon, whose vocal impression of the prime minister was well known in the 1980s thanks to his starring role in *Spitting Image* (ITV, 1984–96). The publicity from the series meant he found himself in demand as an impersonator throughout her tenure as prime minister and beyond. The *Good Morning Britain* caricature was one of many that Nallon performed throughout the 1980s:

> I was on television once or twice a week doing Thatcher on some sort of show. Kids shows, Saturday morning shows, late night. In those days ITV regions on a Friday night would have their own programme for an hour … I was a regular guest on those. (Nallon, 2022)

The kinds of programming Nallon recalls appearing on are what Frances Bonner (2003) calls 'ordinary television'. These are precisely the kinds of everyday, ephemeral programming not designed for repeat, recording or close analysis. Caricature that appears on this kind of programme is especially subject to the 'glance' or 'skim' viewing mode, since these are television shows that assume no special attention on the part of their audiences. The production contexts of programmes of this kind, usually broadcast live or recorded 'as-live', require a great deal of performative flexibility on the part of the impersonator. Nallon (2022) recalled that one of the specialisms that made him an in-demand Thatcher impersonator was the ability to work without a script. Bonner notes that the discursive style most associated with 'ordinary television' is 'chat', arguing that 'there is a superficiality to the exploration of topics on ordinary television, since both intellectual depth and intense emotion … are rare' (2003, 50). Politics and economics, the topics on which the real Thatcher might most regularly be drawn, are among the 'disguised, quarantined and absent' discourses of 'ordinary television' (Bonner, 2003). Nallon uses his improvisational skill to allow his Thatcher caricature to engage in 'chat' appropriate to the magazine format. Guided by hosts Morris and Rustie Lee, 'Thatcher' touches lightly on topical issues relevant to the prime minister, such as her tour of Asia (4–14 April 1985) or a recent bout of flu. Even when asked to respond to Thatcher's recent, controversial comments on British workers, Nallon uses this as an opportunity to make a joke rather than a political point: 'I'm never unfair to the working man in Britain. In fact, I've met him once, a very pleasant man.' While this may be viewed as a trivial comic representation of Thatcher that does not engage in necessary critique, it nevertheless adapts the caricature signature to the specific modality and discursive requirements of the genre on which it appears.

During the segment, 'Thatcher' sits alongside other guests, actors Geraldine McEwan, Jill Bennett and Hawthorne. Though the tone of the conversation between them is tongue-in-cheek, she is referred to throughout as 'Mrs Thatcher' or 'the prime minister'. References to her 'current' tour of Asia reveal a schism between reality and pretence since the prime minister cannot be in two places at once. According to Ferris and Harris, this slippage is common to the 'game' of celebrity impersonation, since these performances 'playfully straddle the line that separates reality from imitation' (2011, 70). Morris questions McEwan on whether she would care to play the prime minister, and 'Thatcher' on whether she would enjoy acting. This line of questioning acknowledges the role-playing that is occurring here and encourages the façade between fiction and reality to slip. The constant shifting between pretence that this is the prime minster, and acknowledgement of the caricature creates an uneven tone for the segment, even as it proceeds in the light-hearted fashion associated with early morning television. The emphasis throughout the segment is on the caricature appearance as a compensation for the absence of the prime minister herself.

Far from an idiosyncratic, decades-old one-off, caricature appearances on magazine and news programming are common in contemporary television. Actor John Di Domenico, who has many credits as a Donald Trump impersonator across film, television, animation and webseries, regularly appears on news and magazine programmes both as a subject of news footage, or in-character bantering with television presenters. For instance, Di Domenico appeared on *Action News*, on local Las Vegas cable news Channel 13 on 19 November 2016, just after Trump's election victory. This segment begins with images of Di Domenico meeting members of the public in character as Trump. An onscreen title reading 'Fake Trump Draws Big Reactions', and a vox pop of a woman who insists she will not have a photograph taken with Trump, real or fake, immediately remove any cause for doubt about the reality-status and purpose of this segment. The caricature is used in this instance to garner public reactions (positive and negative) from Las Vegas residents about the divisive president-elect, with Di Domenico's appearance a comedic spur to responses rather than an attempt to dupe the public. The news anchor and reporter both clearly state that the caricature version of Trump is used as a substitute for these purposes, an 'interesting way' to gauge public reactions. Since Channel 13 had been unable to secure an interview with the real Trump, Di Domenico's caricature is 'the next best thing'.

Many of Di Domenico's televisual appearances act as a comedic substitution in lieu of a formal interview with Trump or another appropriate political figure or commentator. For example, he appeared on Nine Network Australia's *Today* early morning news programme during the October 2020 election campaign, taking part in a 'debate' with a Joe Biden impressionist 'down the line'. Unlike the Channel 13 segment, which clearly indicates that this Trump is a 'fake', *Today*'s onscreen graphics adopt the playful pretence that 'Donald Trump and Joe Biden face off on Today.' Television style is used case to support the 'theatrical frame' that implies a 'sincere imitation', while Di Domenico's performance, in combination with the hosts' amused reactions to it, provide the 'impersonation frame', the cue that this is a comedic and playful set of interactions (Ferris and Harris, 2011). A similar appearance on ITV's *This Morning* on 27 September 2016 (the morning after the first televised presidential debate with Hillary Clinton) superimposes the intertitle 'Exclusive: Donald Trump … Kind of …' over the image of Di Domenico, a use of graphics to gainsay the truth claim of the interview rather than create a theatrical or representational frame for the impersonation (Fig. 2.5).

The segment begins with footage of Trump from the presidential debate, with a scripted introduction by host Holly Willoughby

Fig. 2.5 Phillip Schofield and Holly Willoughby's 'corpsing' sets a playful tone for their interview with 'Donald Trump' (John Di Domenico)

that describes him as 'one of the world's most controversial political figures'; as with *Our Cartoon President,* video provides a real-world comparator against which the caricature can be evaluated. It also uses the conventional grammar of magazine programming flow for introducing new items. While Willoughby's voiceover claims that they are to talk to a 'very special guest', her and co-host Phillip Schofield's laughter upon seeing the made-up Di Domenico constructs an unserious tone. Their corpsing is a presentational cue that frames the segment as humorous even where the content relates to matters with serious and troubling global implications. Corpsing is also, as Karen Lury has argued, an ambivalent gesture that helps to construct television's illusions of reality: 'rather than the corpsing of the performer exposing a breakdown of the system, or an "instance of the unpredictable", such moments are actively promoted as part of the "reality" of the interaction between audience and presenter' (2011, 182). Willoughby and Schofield use the corpsing presentational mode to address the audience with a reassuring wink, letting them in on a joke whose butt is placed at a safe distance. Later, the hosts make the tonally difficult shift to talking to Di Domenico himself, questioning him on making a living from impersonating Trump. Schofield asks to 'speak to John', effectively requesting that Trump is 'switched off'. This is undermined, of course, by Di Domenico remaining in wig, make up and costume that continues to connote Trump-ness. The performance frame is broken down altogether, and the address moves to a more conventional television interview. Willoughby and Schofield's presentational skill means they can handle the shifts in address and performance frame involved in managing a snippet caricature.

Snippet caricature highlights the key problematics of televisual address when confronted by the comedic impersonation: reality versus fiction, presentational versus representational, serious versus unserious, mundane versus extraordinary. Because the kinds of programming on which snippet caricature appears do not have the explicit framing devices of sketch shows, the onus is on the caricature itself, placing pressure on the impersonator to ensure that they are conveying not only the essence of the personality they are portraying, but the caricature-ness of this performance. This must be done with a level of self-consciousness, so that the joke can be passed on easily to an unsuspecting audience member, and to maintain the comic register throughout the performance. Establishing and maintaining this humorous tone is supported in Nallon's Thatcher caricature by the comic incongruity that occurs because she is embodied by a man. Nallon (2022) resisted the label 'drag' in relation to his Thatcher, arguing that he always wanted to keep an element of reality to his impersonation: 'I chose not … to do a drag look, not to exaggerate anything about, myself, and keep it very, very simple, not big.' Actress and impressionist Kate Robbins (2022) corrected my use of the term 'impersonation' to 'impression' during our interview, saying 'I don't know if I feel like a drag act if you say that.' She astutely observes the close overlap between caricature impersonation – an exaggerated, embodied performance of identity – and drag. Drag has a long history on British television, in, for example, the televised cabaret of performers like Danny La Rue or the work of comedian presenters such as Lily Savage or Dame Edna Everage (Bloomfield, 2023). But its most prominent and sustained example, *RuPaul's Drag Race*, presents a notable iteration of – and use for – televisual caricature.

Snatch

RuPaul's Drag Race is a reality competition show in which a group of drag performers compete in a series of weekly challenges to determine who will become the 'next drag superstar', in the vein of host RuPaul Charles, a global drag celebrity. While it began as a low-budget series made for a narrowcast channel (Logo TV) that targeted a specific LGBTQ+ audience, it has grown into a global televisual phenomenon, usually understood to have popularised and mainstreamed drag as an artform (Brennan and Gudelunas, 2023). *Drag Race* has also been franchised in numerous territories such as France, The Netherlands, Brazil, Thailand, Canada, Australia/New Zealand, and the United Kingdom. *RuPaul's Drag Race UK* is made for BBC Three, a channel dedicated not to an identity-focused niche but to a defined demographic of 18- to 34-year-olds. The series retains the original *Drag Race*'s formula elements, irreverent tone and emphasis on themes of relevance to queer communities.[2] It makes appropriate accommodations to its British audience, adopting a somewhat culturally specific sense of humour and set of references. As an extension of the *Drag Race* universe, though, it produces a dual address to a global queer community.

There are substantial intersections between drag, camp and caricature in their shared exploitation of exaggeration, absurdity and satire. Drag is a key popular cultural site of comic impersonation, and it shares with caricature its playful destabilisation of identity via bodily and physiognomic distortions. Drag's status as subversive gender parody has been discussed by feminist and queer scholars, most notably Judith Butler who highlighted its exposure of 'the illusion of gender identity as an intractable depth and inner substance' (1990, 146). Drag can, like other humour forms including caricature, manifest a conservative undercurrent (see Introduction). Just as caricature relies on a shorthand, simplified (occasionally problematic) consensus about the meaning of its target, drag can depend on assumptions about the meanings and value of femininity which need to be tacitly accepted before they can be subverted, that is, if the subversion occurs at all.

Beyond these broader connections between drag and caricature, *Drag Race* has a more specific claim to be an instance of *televisual* caricature. Every season includes an episode, 'Snatch Game', in which the main challenge for the competing drag queens is to appear in a spoof of the TV gameshow *Match Game* (NBC, 1962–). Guest stars are given the beginning of a sentence

---

[2] Its position on the BBC inhibits some typical features of the *Drag Race* formula, for example, the awarding of cash or sponsored prizes for winning challenges, replaced by a 'RuPeter badge'.

to complete in humorous ways to match with a host of 'celebrities' lined up answering the same question. The *Drag Race* twist is that competitors answer questions not as themselves but performing in-character imitations of celebrities. The 'Snatch Game' tests three major skills associated with drag: improvisation, impersonation and wit. Much as drag represents a parody of gender relations, Snatch Game performances are a parody of celebrity identity, and can therefore be seen as queer caricature (Andrews, 2020).

The first Snatch Game episode of *RuPaul's Drag Race UK* (Series One, Episode Four) is of particular interest here because the impersonations bring together our two subjects, Thatcher and Trump. Early in the episode, in a customary sequence in which the queens are shown preparing for their Snatch Game impersonations, controversy breaks out because two contestants have chosen the same character. Baga Chipz reveals her choice as 'Maggie May', delivering Thatcher's famous saying 'the lady's not for turning' in a deep, breathy voice. Divina de Campo has also chosen Thatcher, who she describes as 'probably the most divisive person from British politics ever', before offering her take on the catchphrase. Both Baga and Divina have identified Thatcher's voice and 'lady's not for turning' line as Thatcher's caricature signatures, the key to unlocking near instantaneous identification of the subject. Both have also brought red-blonde bouffant wigs, blue suits and handbags, the key visual identifiers for Thatcher. Members of *Drag Race UK*'s target audience, born after the 1990s, can comfortably be assumed to have only a second-hand knowledge or understanding of Thatcher and her influence. The inclusion of Thatcher as a caricature in this episode, identifiable simply by the name 'Maggie', via a brief vocal impression, or through simple visual markers such as wig and costume, speaks to her ongoing cultural resonance even for those who did not live through her political career. That a competition ensues over the right to 'do Maggie' (which Baga wins when Divina generously cedes the character to her) demonstrates her value as a (queer) caricature subject. This is particularly true in a context in which this caricature must address multiple overlapping audiences, including the young, British audience targeted by the host channel, and a global queer fanbase. Thatcher has meaning even for an audience that may not be intimately familiar with her as a political figure.

During the Snatch Game segment, Baga uses red contact lenses, arched eyebrows and strategically placed lipstick on her teeth to render her Thatcher caricature vampiric. This effect is amplified in her performance, in which she arches her back, neck and shoulders, contorting into an unnatural shape, and delivers her lines in a slow, deliberate pace, mimicking Thatcher's voice (Fig. 2.6). In the tradition of satiric caricature, she uses bodily deformation as part of a moral critique. This monstrous imitation is matched by the assertions made in-character, such as her intention to 'bugger the miners' or give 'more money for the rich less for the poor' (prominent themes in other Thatcher televisual caricatures, such as *Where Am I Now?* and *Psychobitches*). Baga draws on an established tradition for caricaturing Thatcher: abject, grotesque transformation as seen in the caricatures of cartoonists like Steve Bell or Gerald Scarfe, and the burlesque on her real political views. With references to the Belgrano (an Argentine cruiser illicitly sunk during the Falklands War), redundancy and the 'lady's not for turning', Baga's caricature presents an energetic gloss on Thatcher suitable both for the rapid speed of the Snatch Game's structure and editing patterns (Andrews, 2020), and to be easily

Fig. 2.6 Baga Chipz caricatures Margaret Thatcher as a monstrous grotesque, *RuPaul's Drag Race UK*

decoded by a viewer with a limited or superficial knowledge of the subject.

The Vivienne's caricature of Donald Trump goes somewhat against the grain of the Snatch Game, which typically is made up of impersonations of female celebrities, highlighting the commingling of three layers of identity (celebrity identity, drag identity and performer identity).[3] As we have seen, though, Trump has both the easily replicable look and excessive persona that render him a strong candidate for caricature, and for the camp appropriation of drag impersonation. As The Vivienne meets (out of drag) with RuPaul prior to the performance of Snatch Game, she delivers a brief vocal impression of Trump, praised by the host as 'scary' in its accuracy. This highlights first, the uncanny pleasure of hearing a familiar voice emerge from the 'incorrect' body, and second, the incongruity of a drag impersonation of a powerful figure whose hostility to queer people is well known (hence a tongue-in-cheek quip from RuPaul: 'he's not *my* president').

The Vivienne's performance during the Snatch Game segment exploits easily recognisable Trump references – his determination to build a wall on the US's southern border, his boasts of sexual assault against women and accusations of Russian collusion in his election victory – but adds to them camp exaggeration, sexual innuendo and bawdy grotesquery. Her version of Trump exploits the caricature signature visually through costuming, make-up and hair, verbally in the vocal impression, and performatively in the use of hand and facial gestures such as pursed lips and furrowed brow (Fig. 2.7). The impersonation is at once an accurate recreation of an already-extreme political personality, and a comedic exaggeration that calls forth the real Trump's manifold flaws. It relies on the viewer's knowledge of – and shared disposition towards – the president for the references to land and for subversion to take place.

The Snatch Game format, which emphasises the improvisational skill of the competing drag performers, encourages

---

[3] Embodying a male character in the Snatch Game is often presented as a high-risk, high-reward strategy.

Fig. 2.7 The Vivienne's caricature of Donald Trump replicates the president's signature facial and bodily gestures, *RuPaul's Drag Race UK*

extemporised exchanges. The unpredictability of how this miscellaneous group of caricatures will interact is central to the pleasure the Snatch Game offers its audience. The game adopts the playful impersonation frame Ferris and Harris (2011) identify, with frequent self-conscious references to the impossibility of the represented scenario.[4] These are presentational caricatures that are nevertheless embedded in an acknowledged fictional context. This provides fertile ground for comic scenarios, for example, a flirtation between the Thatcher and Trump, against the logic of time:

> Trump/Vivienne: This woman's an inspiration. If anyone knew how to fuck up a country, it's her.
> Thatcher/Baga: I love you too, but please, keep those orange cheesy balls away from my face.

Within this short dialogue, the possibilities of (queer) televisual caricature are revealed. The Vivienne uses the opportunity of putting words in the mouth of Trump to satirical ends. In aligning

---

[4] For instance, it has become a trope for Snatch Game caricatures to refer to the fact that the depicted subject is dead.

Trump and Thatcher through the discourse of 'inspiration', she proposes an implicit critique of right-wing populism and its (in her view) disastrous effects. Baga, on the other hand, uses her Thatcher caricature apolitically, crafting humour instead from the shocking incongruity of hearing the words 'orange cheesy balls' escaping the lips of a politician who famously took herself very seriously. Camp exaggeration and grotesquery are employed in the service of a satire that, while contained by the entertainment format it appears in, retains its bite.

Both Baga and Vivienne queer their caricature subjects, presenting a camp subversion of these figureheads of the political right. The 'iconic' status of Thatcher has led to her re-appropriation as an unlikely gay icon in the years after her term as prime minister (Coleman, 2007). Paul Philip Flynn (2006) suggests this relates to both her 'strong, identifiable signature look' – evidenced by the ease with which a blue power suit and a red-blonde teased wig can connote 'Thatcherness' – and her 'camp, easily cartooned presence', a descriptor that could also refer to Trump. Dominic Janes notes that the queering of Thatcher is ambivalent:

> For some observers the exploitation of the cultural complexity of Thatcher as a public figure in order to allow her to be represented in a manner that overrides the significance of her political actions can be regarded as an impressive act of queering. But for others such cultural manipulation represents nothing more than a dangerous distortion of the historical record that threatens to overwrite the attitudes and experiences of those gay men and women who were bitterly opposed to Thatcherism. (2012, 225)

In presenting a queer caricature of Thatcher, then, Baga continues this tradition of reappraisals of her as a cultural figure, in which, as Louisa Hadley and Elizabeth Ho (2010) argue, the Thatcher persona becomes a powerful *obstacle* that occludes proper engagement with the political meaning of Thatcher*ism*. Caricatures of Thatcher may thus close down rather than enhance critiques of her politics. Similar arguments have been offered about the caricature of Donald Trump; to satirise him is to reproduce the mediated self-parody he created, humanising him rather than offering effective critique (Howell and Parry-Giles, 2018; Becker, 2021). These queer caricatures therefore suggest we might consider a further tension in televisual caricature. Though they might perform the satirical function of critiquing political figures, their subversions are contained within the denigration of an individual and the exaggeration of their flaws, which means that they can only allude to, rather than engage fully, with the systemic oppressions that these figures metonymically represent.

Conclusion

Televisual caricatures are incursions into everyday television programming. Sometimes we find them where we might expect to, for instance in sketch comedy, impressions shows, animations. We are cued, in these cases, to anticipate a comedic impersonation that does what caricatures do: that highlights character traits through their exaggeration, and in doing so provide an externalisation of the putative flaws of the public figure. In the cases of the Thatcher and Trump caricatures analysed in this chapter, the most common mode of address undertaken in these caricatures is one that assumes a knowing audience, one with a sceptical disposition to their target. The 'preferred reading' encoded in these caricatures is a critical, oppositional or negotiated one. Televisual caricatures can also crop up and take us unawares, an unexpected jolt of grotesque distortion, a figure we half recognise, the comic underscore of everyday political and popular culture. They playfully traverse the boundaries between representational and presentational performance styles, and between illusion and reality, constructing the 'impersonation frame' that enables the temporary suspension of disbelief alongside a decoding of references to real events and characteristics relevant to the caricature.

Televisual form complements the role of caricature as a public, popular and ephemeral mode. It addresses 'silly citizens', armed with knowledge and understanding of the public figure sufficient to enable distorted recognition to take place, and to find pleasure (or at least amusement) in the ridicule. Televisual caricatures can operate as tools somewhere between the 'cultural public sphere', which engages fictions to support an emotional response to the moral dilemmas of the everyday lives of citizens, and the 'comic public sphere', which parodies the conventions of the normative public sphere to encourage critical reflection on the powerful people, institutions and discourses that occupy it. The exaggerations of caricature, coupled with television's well-established conventions for addressing a 'glancing' audience, enable it to rise above the noise, and direct our attention, even if fleetingly, to the absurdities of power and those who practise it.

This chapter has explored the relationship between caricature form and televisual address. It has examined televisual caricature's combination of textual elements, including aesthetics (visual and graphic design, performance style, sound) and structure (generic form, narrative style), paratextual elements (scheduling, title sequences, interstitials) and contextual elements (political and institutional). Together, these frame the televisual caricature and show how it encourages viewers to adopt a certain subject position and critical disposition towards its target, its liminal placement at the boundary between fact and fiction, and its adoption of discourses appropriate to genre and form in which it appears. What has not yet been considered, however, is how caricature fits into the context of television as the product of a creative industry: how television's commercial, political and cultural imperatives come together in the making of televisual caricature. I will turn my attention in this direction in Chapter 3.

3
Making Televisual Caricature

Introduction

Some readers may have noticed an obvious absence in the last chapter's case study of Thatcher televisual caricatures: *Spitting Image* (ITV, 1984–96), a puppet-based sketch programme that was the dominant political satire on British television throughout the 1980s and early 1990s. Made of latex and voiced by impressionist Steve Nallon (see Chapter 2), *Spitting Image*'s Thatcher appeared in every episode until her resignation as Prime Minister in November 1990. This 'Thatcher' adopted – indeed, prefigured – many elements of the caricature signature identified in Chapter 2: the low, mellifluous voice, delivered in syncopated rhythm, the syrupy but sinister tone of speech, the tendency towards sudden, angry outbursts, the strawberry blonde coiffured wig, the masculinising costume of boxy, tailored suits and the aggressively wielded handbag. Transforming Thatcher into a caricature puppet enabled grotesque exaggerations of her physiognomic features, especially piercing eyes, darkened, downturned lips and a long, sharp nose, to act as proxy accusations of monstrosity. She is at once matronly and militaristic, sweet and steely, but *always* in charge (unless, that is, President Reagan is around).

Spitting Image has achieved an almost mythological status in popular British television history, which makes the relative scarcity of in-depth scholarship on the show rather odd. Its frequent inclusion as archive footage in documentary programming about British politics, culture and TV in the 1980s displays the show's centrality to the cultural imaginary of this period.[1] The most repeated sketch usefully encapsulates *Spitting Image*'s tone and style.[2] In it, Thatcher and members of her cabinet are out to dinner. A waitress addresses her, as is customary for *Spitting Image*, as 'sir' and asks for her order. Thatcher chooses a raw steak; what else, for this apex predator? When asked 'what about the vegetables?' she responds with casual cruelty and an insouciant wave of her rubber hand, 'Oh, they'll have the same as me' (Fig. 3.1). So embedded into popular memory has this sketch become that in March 2024, a former Conservative advisor appeared on the GB News television channel and described this scene as though an anecdote about the real Thatcher, a not unusual mnemonic fusion of puppet and prime minister (Patrick, 2024). The show has been credited with cementing Thatcher's 'Iron Lady' reputation in the 1980s and beyond (Farr, 2018) and has certainly had an indelible influence on subsequent media portrayals. *Spitting Image*'s Thatcher has a fair claim to be the best-known and most influential example of televisual caricature.

This chapter departs somewhat from previous studies of *Spitting Image*, which have approached the series as a remediation of traditions of visual satire (Brillenburg Wurth, 2011), as a parody of televisual genre (Meinhof and Smith, 2000) or as a development of the British satirical tradition (Wagg, 1992). Rather than offering a textual reading of the series, I focus on the making of *Spitting Image*. Drawing on a range of archives, interviews with personnel and content analyses, I discuss the commissioning, production and dissemination practices that brought the show about, and the industrial contexts that shaped them.[3]

---

[1] Examples include *Maggie & Me* (Channel 4, 2013), *The 80s: Ten Years That Changed Britain* (Channel 4, 2016), *The 80s With Dominic Sandbrook* (BBC Two, 2016) and *1984: Most Shocking Moments* (Channel 5, 2024). There are many others.
[2] This sketch originally aired as a post-end-credits scene on 20 January 1985.
[3] The archives consulted were Roger Law Collection, Cambridge University Library; Independent Broadcasting Authority archive, Bournemouth

Fig. 3.1 The 'Vegetables' sketch, *Spitting Image*

In doing so, I evaluate televisual caricature as TV content in two periods of radical change. *Spitting Image* first aired during an era in which the Conservative government's media policies precipitated a long realignment of the UK television industry away from public service and toward market-based imperatives. One clear signal of this change was the growth of the independent television production sector, of which Spitting Image Productions,

---

University Library; British Film Institute; and Media Archive for Central England. Personnel interviewed included Roger Law, Peter Fluck, Charles Denton, Jon Blair, John Lloyd, Doug Naylor, Steve Nallon, Jan Ravens and Kate Robbins. Content analysis was undertaken on the first twelve series of the programme, using the commercially released DVD box set. Sketch lengths were measured in seconds. Sketch content was categorised as: Parody, Political, Celebrity (including royal family), Song, Sport and Other. The puppets that appeared in each sketch and details of their identity (including gender, ethnicity and role in public life) were recorded. Thanks to John Sandy-Hindmarch for undertaking this work. The dataset is available from the University of Lincoln repository (Andrews and Sandy-Hindmarch, 2024).

the company that made the programme, was a part. Though the series has been proposed and perceived as, in the words of creator Roger Law, 'public service satire', it also resulted from the commercial logics of the television industry in the 1980s. In 2020, *Spitting Image* came back after nearly twenty-five years away from British screens. The industry into which it was reintroduced had been transformed in the age of 'Peak TV', a term coined by FX Networks chief John Landgraf in 2015 to capture the sense that television content production had reached an unsustainable critical mass (Littleton, 2015). In this period, a surfeit of audiovisual content has presented an existential threat both to broadcast TV as a medium and TV institutions that primarily serve national audiences. In this context, streaming service Britbox adopted the reboot as attention-grabbing content, intended to offer a unique selling point to entice new subscribers, and to cut through the competition from a range of other video-on-demand providers. This chapter examines the making of *Spitting Image*'s original and reboot series in these distinct contexts, illuminating the industrial role of televisual caricature. Televisual caricature meant something different to the television industry in each of these periods. This chapter will detail what this 'something' was.

Spitting Image and industrial change in the 1980s and 1990s

The origins of *Spitting Image*

Spitting Image began with the caricature art of its originators, Peter Fluck and Roger Law, who met at Cambridge School of Art in the late 1950s. Their teacher, Paul Hogarth, was an early influence who, according to Law, 'demonstrat[ed] the possibilities for combining art with action', while also impressing them with his ability to make a decent living by selling his work in the marketplace (Law et al., 1992, 19–20). The combination of political art and entrepreneurialism would characterise their later work as caricaturists and on *Spitting Image*. Luck and Flaw, their working partnership, formed in 1976, specialising in grotesque, three-dimensional caricature models. These were photographed for publications such as the *Sunday Times*, *Der Spiegel* and *Newsweek*. High production costs limited the profitability of this enterprise. Changes taking place in the newspaper industry, with the arrival of commercially minded moguls like Rupert Murdoch, meant that commissions were becoming rarer (Fluck, 2022; Law, 2022). Fluck and Law therefore sought alternative income streams. Law (2022) recalled that 'the obvious thing to do was to make the three- dimensional things move. It wasn't a stroke of genius; it was a necessity.'

Graphic designer Martin Lambie-Nairn is usually credited with introducing the idea of creating a television programme as a vehicle for these moving caricatures. In 1982, his company, Robinson Lambie-Nairn, provided £2,500 seed-funding for research and development into translating the model caricatures into moving bodies, and he began to enquire into how to assemble and sell a TV programme (Chester, 1986, 10–11).[4] The method for doing this outside of the BBC or regional ITV companies at this time was not obvious, because there was little precedent for it. The independent television production sector was a small 'cottage industry', and companies had limited access either to finance or to television airtime, unless they had pre-established contacts within the major broadcasters (Darlow, 2004; Potter, 2008). Although the establishment of Channel 4 in 1982 marked a sea change in the sector, given its explicit purpose of broadcasting programming from independents, it would take more than a decade for the sector to scale up and for commissioning processes to formalise.

Fluck and Law joined with Tony Hendra, a satirist who had previously commissioned Luck and Flaw work for the *National Lampoon*, to form a production company. Needing partners with 'television credibility', in Fluck's words (2022), they recruited John Lloyd, a BBC comedy producer who had a hit with *Not the*

---

[4] Computer entrepreneur Clive Sinclair also lent £10,000.

Nine O'clock News (BBC Two, 1979–82). Lloyd had previously approached Fluck and Law about providing short caricature inserts into the programme, an idea that proved prohibitively expensive (Lloyd, 2022). Jon Blair, who had built a successful freelance career in current affairs, completed the team, as operational manager. Both Jo(h)ns took equity in the company in lieu of payment. The working relationship between the five men was fractious from the beginning, with competing creative visions for the television programme and a level of territorialism over their roles in the company (Chester, 1986).

Blair's freelancing experience led him to conclude that the best route for televising Fluck and Law's caricatures was to operate as an independent production company, though he quickly realised that the level of funding required to produce a puppet caricature show would necessitate a partnership with an existing television network (Blair, 2022). In late 1982, he and Lloyd took a dossier outlining the project, at this point called 'Spit N Image', to potential broadcast partners. It contained postcard images of existing Luck and Flaw caricatures, biographies of the personnel involved, a short introduction and a description of the intended format. The proposed structure for the show was a hybrid between a sketch show and a sitcom, featuring recurring caricatures fulfilling specific narrative roles, and repeated joke scenarios (such as 'Breakfast with the Brezhnevs'), which was Hendra's preferred format. The brochure outlines an explicit aim to combine puppetry with Luck and Flaw caricature, with a stress on their satirical purpose beyond providing an amusing likeness of their subject. To convey the televisual potential of the project, the pamphlet explains that the scenarios in which Luck and Flaw caricatures are photographed will be translated for television via the imitation of genres like soap opera, cop shows and historical drama. It posits that the combination of puppet caricature with pre-existing TV formats is a winning formula for a commercial television programme (Spit 'n' Image Productions, 1982). Many of the ideas presented in the proposal are recognisable in the programme that would eventuate.

The project was turned down by London Weekend Television, Thames and the BBC. Channel 4, only a few months old, would have been a good political and aesthetic fit, with its determination to provide an alternative view to the mainstream and to innovate in the content and style of programmes. But it had insufficient budget to afford the high production costs for *Spitting Image*, and it was too early in its life to take such a significant financial (and political) risk. One broadcaster had the right combination of capital to invest, a desire to try innovative programming as part of a broader agenda to revamp its image and an adventurous commissioner. This was Central Independent Television, one of the 'big five' ITV franchise-holders that were responsible for providing the bulk of programming to the national network. ITV franchises were (until 1990) awarded every few years by the Independent Broadcasting Authority (IBA), the regulator and operator of the network, through an application process. In the 1980 franchise round, Associated Television (ATV), the broadcaster in the lucrative Midlands area, was compelled to change its ownership structure and identity to recognise the cultural character and 'business patterns' of the region (Bonner and Aston, 1988, 11). ATV was restructured and rebranded as Central in January 1982. Central wanted programming that could change its reputation as a purveyor of light entertainment and low-quality drama. Its Controller of Programmes was Charles Denton, a believer in 'creative mischief' who was keen to shake up Central's offer, change its image and 'make its output much more noisy' (Denton, 2023). Though *Spitting Image*'s cost had dissuaded other broadcasters, Denton used his considerable autonomy at Central to pursue this unique television project with the potential to make a lot of noise. After a successful 20-minute pilot (with the working title of 'The Late Latex Show') was produced in June 1983, Denton enthusiastically commissioned *Spitting Image* for a series to be broadcast in February 1984.

Making *Spitting Image*

The production of *Spitting Image* was a complex affair, requiring the input of writers, producers, caricaturists, designers, mould-makers, foam rubber mixers, costumers, wig stylists, studio personnel, directors, puppeteers, voice actors, composers, audio engineers, the Central board and the regulator, the IBA. These various participants needed to be wrangled in a cyclical weekly process that saw up to three episodes' worth of material being produced in parallel. Caricature's demand for topicality and ever-present potential for controversy put pressure on the whole system. The cycle began with scripts. Writing was supplied by a range of freelancers, some of whom were commissioned to produce a certain proportion of material per show, and some who sent in unsolicited sketches (Lloyd, 2022). Hendra was initially responsible for script editing, and his preferences for how the show should be constructed included longer sketches, running jokes and a surreal tone. He championed, for example, the sitcom-style series of sketches 'Exchequers', set in a retirement home populated by previous prime ministers, and, bizarrely, presided over by Queen Victoria (Fig. 3.2). Hendra's vision was at odds with the rest of the team, and these creative (and personal) differences saw him leave the project after six episodes. Blair recruited young writers Rob Grant and Doug Naylor to replace him, with a generous pay offer (Naylor, 2022). They worked with Lloyd to change the format of the programme, dispensing with recurring features, making sketches shorter, and including more caricatures from the world of celebrity, popular culture and sport. 'Exchequers' was excised.

As script editors, Grant and Naylor reversed the system by which sketches were constructed around the existing puppets, effectively requiring that new models be created to 'service a sketch' (Naylor, 2022). These creative decisions had cost implications, since more caricatures and shorter sketches required the production of more sets, costumes, props and, of course, puppets. This added extra pressure to the workshop, which could generate only around three puppets per week. The manufacture of the

Fig. 3.2 Exchequers sketch, *Spitting Image*

puppets, from the design of the caricatures on the page to the mixing and setting of the foam rubber and latex, was an arduous process and a large sunk cost, reported at between £5,000 and £15,000 each (Knight, 1986, 9). The workshop would eventually develop a production-line technique Law sardonically described as the 'world's first caricature sweatshop' in a BBC *Omnibus* documentary, filmed in 1985. Salaries for workers in the workshop were generous, to compensate for unusually long working hours (Fluck, 2022; Law, 2022). It was housed in a former banana warehouse in London's Canary Wharf. The area, previously docklands, was undergoing regeneration thanks to being designated an 'Enterprise Zone' by the Thatcher government. Spitting Image Productions benefitted from tax and rate exemptions, as well as looser building regulations which would aid the refurbishment of the caricature 'factory'. Government regulations designed to encourage entrepreneurship and growth would ironically create the conditions for some of Thatcher's most visible critics to scale up their operation.

The puppets' voices were supplied by impressionists, who recorded their lines in Central's Birmingham studios, on the set used for soap opera *Crossroads* (ITV, 1964–88). Actors Jan Ravens (2022) and Kate Robbins (2022) both compared this with making a radio programme, reading lines directly from scripts which enabled a speedier recording process. Actors typically supplied voices without having seen the puppet beforehand (aside from recurring characters such as the royal family or politicians), which required them to develop a performance based on their own experience and comic interpretation of the subject. Steve Nallon (2022), who was both a voice actor and puppeteer on the show, recalled being discouraged by the producers from performing accurate impressions, and to consider himself instead a 'vocal caricaturist'. As Robbins (2022) put it, 'it's not just a question of getting the voice, it's making them *funny*'. As with other roles in the production of *Spitting Image*, impressionists were paid well for their labour (Robbins, 2022). Both Ravens and Robbins described working on the programme as fun, though also noted that the availability of work for them as actors was limited by the lack of representation for women on the programme. Between 1984 and 1990, the average proportion of male to female puppets in sketches was 82 to 18 per cent. One third of the appearances by any female puppet between 1984 and 1990 represented a single subject, Margaret Thatcher, who was voiced by a man. Though there were key women working on the series, including expert puppeteer Louise Gold, and producer Joanna Beresford, who became Managing Director of Spitting Image Ltd in January 1991, it was an undeniably male-dominated working environment.

Spitting Image was co-produced between Spitting Image Productions and Central as a 'package', which meant it was made with Central's production facilities and personnel. Filming took place in Central's Birmingham studios, according to Ian Potter 'almost certainly … so that the company could absorb those costs internally as below the line expenditure' (2008, 133). This added extra logistical complexity, as producers, performers and puppets had to be ferried between London and Birmingham on a weekly basis. Production for a series of *Spitting Image* would begin several weeks before the first episode aired. Writers, puppeteers, impressionists and production personnel would be engaged for 'banking', that is, recording general sketches to be included in the new series that could be produced in advance. 'Topicals', segments of the show that satirised recent events, were written (until 1988) by satirical partnership Nick Newman and Ian Hislop, on a Friday afternoon or Saturday morning to enable a review of the week's news cycle (Naylor, 2022). These would amount to only a few minutes an episode but were crucial in creating the show's reputation for cutting-edge satire. Voice recordings generally took place on a Saturday, while last-minute filming occurred on Sundays, with edits often taking place perilously close to the 10 p.m. airtime for the show. This relentless, seven-day schedule took its toll on the producers, especially Lloyd. He recalled working on one series for ninety consecutive days (Lloyd, 2022). He, understandably, could not sustain this working pattern, and left Spitting Image Productions in 1987. Though there were many other personnel changes, the production methods for *Spitting Image* remained consistent. This complex system was expensive. The first series was estimated to cost £2.6m, a large budget even for high-end drama in 1984 (ITV News, 2014).

Production was complicated further in the first series by negotiations between producers, broadcaster and regulator about the show's content. Denton (2023) foresaw 'an enormous amount of legal faffing about' over *Spitting Image*. The IBA was, predictably, cautious about this provocative programme. Because the show was pre-recorded, IBA personnel could exercise a certain degree of control over its content, and the Authority decided in January 1984 to preview at least the first few episodes (IBA, 1984a). This gave the IBA, Central and Spitting Image Productions the opportunity to establish the parameters of acceptability through negotiation. For example, on 29 February 1984, Denton wrote to the IBA querying its requested cuts to language and some physical comedy involving the puppet of Harold Macmillan (Denton, 1984). He reminded the Authority that the figures are just puppets and should therefore not be taken as seriously as a straightforward impersonation. This was a rhetorical appeal to televisual caricature's place in the cultural public sphere, in which fiction endows television programming greater licence for political contestation (see Chapter 2). Lloyd met with IBA officers prior to the broadcast of the first six episodes, tasked with justifying the jokes and, in his words, 'persuading them that I was a responsible adult' (Lloyd, 2022). After this initial teething period, relations between Spitting Image Productions, Central and IBA settled into a détente, with a level of mutual understanding about the tolerable limits of provocation. Though there would be various controversies throughout the life of *Spitting Image*, the IBA routinely defended the programme against its critics.

The IBA's concerns about *Spitting Image* were largely not legal ones but centred on its propensity to poor taste. Nowhere was this more evident than the regulator's worries about how the show would depict the British royal family. The 'royals' problem would become clear from its very first episode, which aired on 26 February 1984. At a late stage in its production, Denton called Fluck, Law, Lloyd, Blair and Hendra into his office to deliver some bad news. Central's board had requested the removal of any references to the royal family, which amounted to more than a fifth of its 25-minute runtime. This was viewed by some in the team as an act of flagrant censorship, and there were disagreements as to whether to comply or to withdraw the series from production altogether. Eventually it was decided to deliver a shorter episode than had been commissioned (Chester, 1986, 65–9). It soon became apparent that there was no mandate from Central to censor all material about the royal family. It was a matter of inconvenient timing: the Duke of Edinburgh was due to open Central's new studios in Nottingham on 2 March 1984, and the board wanted to avoid embarrassment. In the event, he evidently had a sense of humour about *Spitting Image*, joking with the press that they were seeing him, not the puppet (Media Archive for Central England, undated). It is not surprising that he was already aware of *Spitting Image*. Central's press office had actively generated hype for the series from December 1983, exploiting the curiosity and controversy an untried concept like puppet caricature TV naturally excited (Chester, 1986, 59).

The Duke of Edinburgh's joke unconsciously prefigured what would become a signature humour style for *Spitting Image*: playful, self-conscious irony. This manifested in its intertextual parody of television genre and style (Meinhof and Smith, 2000), but also in the self-referential use of caricature. A good example related to the royal family appeared in the episode that aired 24 February 1985. The episode concludes with a fade to a black screen, on which, in a stern white font, is written 'SPITTING IMAGE: A statement'. A voiceover, read in solemn tones by actor Chris Barrie, can be heard as text scrolls on screen, in a parody of the standard format for television retractions or regulator-mandated apologies. It says:

> It has been widely reported in the newspapers that a so-called 'puppet' of the Queen Mother would appear on this week's programme. To the press, the public, and the many members of parliament who have kindly rung in to complain, we would like to admit that this was an outrageous and contemptible untruth perpetrated by us, to bring the programme into line with current government policy guidelines.
>
> Spitting Image have never made such a puppet and were on holiday at the time it wasn't made.
>
> Thank you.

As the text fades, the screen remains blank for a moment. A caricature puppet wanders into the right of frame. It is unmistakably the Queen Mother, signified through her costume of a dusky pink coat, white gloves and lace-fronted, feathered hat, all of which featured in her usual public wardrobe. She says, in a high pitched, plummy tone 'what a pity. And I was so looking forward to it', while the puppet meets the eye of the viewer in direct address (Fig. 3.3). In contrast to the feared disrespectful or cruel caricature of this much-loved public figure, this was a gentle introduction to the show for the Queen Mother, who would later appear sporadically in the series, in a much less flattering depiction.

Fig. 3.3 The Queen Mother makes her first appearance on *Spitting Image*

This joke captures something of *Spitting Image*'s place in the cultural public sphere. It demonstrates the peculiar sensitivity of the British press, government and public to caricature depictions of the royal family, and the propensity for the show to generate public disapproval. But it also acknowledges (with irony) the active role played by Spitting Image Productions in developing a mutually beneficial relationship with the press. Lloyd (2022) described this thus: 'if you give them a good story, they'll be your friend, and so we had great stories, particularly for the tabloids'. While much of the journalistic coverage of *Spitting Image* – especially its depiction of the royals – was negative, it nevertheless provided effective publicity for the series. As Denton (2023) pointed out, attention from the press, even in the form of critique, was essential: 'to do a show like that which had anarchic ambitions, and then to have a soggy, totally unresponsive press would have been catastrophic'.

Although the depictions of the royal family were gentler than other figures satirised on *Spitting Image*, they generated the most press attention, and consequently the most complaints. Minutes of a 16 January 1985 meeting of the IBA noted that the series often 'sailed close to the wind' in its depictions of the royal family (IBA, 1985), though the authority was robust in their responses to complaints from members of the public and members of parliament about *Spitting Image*. A typical argument was to justify the programme's provocations with reference to the role that satire has played in British cultural life, comparing *Spitting Image* with the work of Jonathan Swift and respected satirical revue *That Was the Week That Was* (BBC Television, 1962–3). As televisual caricature, *Spitting Image* became defensible as the inheritor of this tradition, a rhetorical stance that the IBA and Spitting Image Productions team would repeat numerous times during the series broadcast (IBA, 1984b, 1986a, 1987; Hislop, 1988).

Given its flagship status and high level of promotion, initial audiences of six to seven million viewers were disappointing, if healthy for a 10 p.m. Sunday timeslot (Chester, 1986, 95). The decision to schedule in this 'graveyard' slot was strategic. Denton wanted the show in a post-watershed position to allow for grotesque imagery, adult language and controversial themes. It had the added benefit of being a risk-reduced space to try an experimental programme, since ratings expectations would be lower than peak time. The economics of the ITV network were such that the high profitability of Central's overall portfolio meant that it would be able to swallow a significant loss if *Spitting Image* flopped. In any case, the purpose of the series was as much to bring attention and prestige to Central as it was to generate large audiences. There is evidence of its success in this. For example, in the IBA's 1985 Yearbook (Melaniphy, 1984, 203) a photograph of the Mick Jagger puppet illustrates Central's dedicated page, the image chosen to represent the company's entire yearly output. Indicating its growing significance to the ITV network, *Spitting Image* commands more space in the 1986 yearbook, with an entire feature on the show, and a full-page photograph of the John Gielgud puppet (Melaniphy, 1985, 106–7). A newspaper advertisement for Central from November 1986 cites *Spitting Image* as an 'innovative comedy' that 'extends the frontiers of satirical humour', signifying Central's commitment to the 'highest quality of programming' (Central Television, 1986). It is difficult to determine the average overall audience for *Spitting Image*. The claim of a regular audience of 15m viewers appears strikingly often in retrospective discussion of the series, whether in the documentary programming previously mentioned, or journalism (for example, BBC News, 2019a; Pelley, 2020). It has not been possible to substantiate this figure. If *Spitting Image* were gaining 15m viewers in the 1980s, it would have sat comfortably near the top of ITV's ten highest-rated television programmes in any given week, which at this time received between 11m and 17m viewers. A 'Top Ten' list of ITV ratings, with figures obtained from the Broadcasters Audience Research Board, was published regularly in *The Times* Information Service pages throughout the 1980s. *Spitting Image* appears only once in this list, with 14.25m viewers (ITV's fourth highest audience that week) in March 1986 (*The Times*, 1986, 20). Given this evidence, we can conclude that the audience for the show did not regularly exceed 11m. To do so, in any case, with a provocative comedy in a late evening slot on a Sunday, would have been somewhat miraculous. A brochure produced by Spitting Image Productions (undated, but likely from early 1988) puts the figure for the Autumn 1987 series at 'over 8m', a realistic average for the show (Spitting Image Productions, undated a).

The demographic make up of the audience was significant. When Denton commissioned *Spitting Image*, he hoped it 'might attract an audience which wasn't around in ITV terms, at the time, which was younger-skewed' (Denton, 2023). It was indeed watched by large numbers of younger viewers: the Spitting Image Productions brochure suggests a figure of 3.5m 25- to 45-year-olds for Autumn 1987 (Spitting Image Productions, undated a). The show's popularity with young people became an important defence for the IBA. For example, an IBA regional officer replied to a complaint thus:

> *Spitting Image* seems to be carving out an extremely loyal and sizeable audience for itself among the under-35s

> according to our figures. I know from my own conversations with people in this age group that they are less offended by vulgarity and references to the Royal Family.
> (IBA, 1986b)

The audience was also disproportionately of the ABC1 socioeconomic group, that is, the professional middle class. Even as the series was coming to an end, in 1994, it still delivered an estimated 2.08m ABC1 adults to ITV, around 40 per cent of the programme's total audience (*The Times*, 1994, 22). Regardless of the actual size and make up of *Spitting Image*'s audience, its cultural ubiquity was undeniable. Its influence may have originated in its position as televisual caricature, but it would become something bigger.

Spitting Image beyond British TV

Expanding beyond the bounds of a half-hour television show and into the centre of popular and political culture helped *Spitting Image* to maintain its relevance and importance to the British zeitgeist. This is reflected in the regularity with which the puppets would feature as the image to accompany news stories about politics in place of photographs of the politicians. One of many examples appears in a November 1992 *Times* cover story about European Union negotiations over tariffs (Bishop, 1992). Chancellor Norman Lamont and Prime Minister John Major are portrayed using a photograph of a *Spitting Image*–themed Christmas display at the London department store Liberty, in which the puppets are made up as pantomime characters. As highlighted in Chapter 2, televisual caricatures can offer a comic substitute for the real persona or image. That the puppets appear in the Liberty display also demonstrates their contradictory commercial use. *Spitting Image* puppets made regular 'personal appearances' at professional events. In the late 1980s, Spitting Image Production's Engineering subdivision developed specialist computational animatronics, a system called 'Flexator', that enabled the puppets to interact with participants. A promotional pamphlet (Spitting Image Productions, undated b), produced around 1990, advertises this use of the puppets for a range of purposes including trade fairs, exhibitions, TV commercials, political rallies and AGMs. It claims that the animatronic system enables the puppets to appear with no human interference aside from writing a cheque. This tongue-in-cheek reference to the commercialisation of *Spitting Image* presents a level of ironic detachment to the expansion of the brand beyond television.

The animatronic caricatures, rather like the television puppets, were envisaged as an extension of the 3D caricaturing of Luck and Flaw (Fluck, 2022). The research and development costs were substantial, and corporate uses for the technology were a means to recoup them. Another proposed use for the moving puppets was as part of a visitor attraction called the 'World of Spitting Image', mooted as early as 1987, and reported in the *London Standard* in February 1988. The idea of an exhibition displaying Luck and Flaw caricatures predated the television show, a helpful reminder that the expansion of *Spitting Image* beyond television should be viewed as an extension of a pre-existing cross-media brand, albeit one that was not explicitly conceived on these terms. While the planned large attraction did not materialise, an exhibition called the 'Spitting Image Rubberworks', a Madame Tussauds–style display, opened in Covent Garden in London on 15 December 1990. In 1991, it attracted 200,000 visitors (Young, 1992). It was highlighted in tourist information produced by the London Underground as late as May 1993 (London Underground, 1993). Of the Rubberworks, Fluck (2022) noted that though he spent a lot of energy pursuing it as an idea, the 'budgets didn't work', and that it required topicality and creativity at a similar level to the TV show, but without the guaranteed income of a television commission.

In addition to the extra-televisual appearance of the puppets, the development of various kinds of *Spitting Image* merchandise helped to sustain its brand well into the 1990s. At least initially, though, licensing was not part of a conscious strategy on the part of the programme team and operated on an ad hoc basis. Decisions about merchandising appear to have been motivated by personal gratification more than commercial considerations. For instance, when the team were approached about the 'Pet Hates' dog toy range, Law agreed on the basis that he found the proposition amusing, and on the proviso that they would be sold only in pet stores. Other examples of licensed material included books, records, a board game, a computer game and answering machine tapes with recordings by *Spitting Image* impressionists.

Lloyd, who had experience of successfully merchandising with *Not the Nine O'clock News*, believed that Spitting Image Productions could have done further commercial exploitation but did not because 'it was considered a sell-out' (2022). Law, for example, described tie-in record 'The Chicken Song' as an 'embarrassment' (2022). The song was written by Phil Pope, from lyrics by Grant and Naylor, who, reflecting that some of the songs that had already appeared in the show were good enough to be records, set out to write a number one single. They parodied disco-friendly pop hits by the group Black Lace, with lyrics infused with *Spitting Image*'s trademark irony and absurdity. Naylor (2022) recalled wanting to 'write something *really* annoying, and that will be really catchy, and *tell* people it will be really catchy but they'll still buy it'. The record was at number one in the UK charts for three weeks in May 1986. This allowed an opportunity for further TV cross-promotion: an appearance on the chart countdown show *Top of the Pops* (BBC, 1964–2022; Fig. 3.4). The performance afforded viewers the surreal (and undeniably laughable) image of Ronald Reagan and Margaret Thatcher puppets dressed as holiday entertainers waving rubber chickens to the beat of a silly, extremely contagious song. *Spitting Image* puppets also made their mark on music television via their starring role in the video for Genesis single 'Land of Confusion', released in November 1986. This featured regularly on MTV in the US, then the UK after the launch of MTV Europe in August 1987.

Fig. 3.4 *Spitting Image* puppets appear on *Top of the Pops* to promote 'The Chicken Song'

'The Chicken Song' – a parody of an irritating pop hit that itself became an irritating pop hit – is a fitting metaphor for the commercialisation of *Spitting Image* more broadly. Though most of the tie-in merchandise maintains the television programme's tone of aloof comic detachment, it nevertheless engaged in the capitalistic exploitation of a brand asset. A 1990 article in *The Listener* on the commercial expansion of *Spitting Image* summarised the ambivalent position of the team:

> Most of [them] were implacably opposed to Thatcherism and despised the ethos of the 'enterprise culture'. Necessarily, therefore, many of the key personnel resisted indiscriminate cashing in on the show's success … both the writers and the workshop tend[ed] to regard satirising and selling as incompatible. (Dugdale, 1990, 15)

This assessment was written on the cusp of change at the company, perhaps most clearly manifested in the decision to allow the puppets to be used in British television adverts for companies such as Woolworths and Bank of Scotland. The end of the 1980s and early 1990s saw a more concerted effort on the part of Spitting Image Productions to exploit its commercial potential. A brochure advertising licensing opportunities for the show states that 'the TV series was only the beginning', describing the company as 'without doubt one of the success stories of Thatcher's Britain' (Spitting Image Productions, undated a). While clearly humorous in tone, these commercial claims sit incongruously with its purpose of ridiculing the political and cultural elites. The commercialisation of *Spitting Image* was ambivalent for its creators, who were conscious of the risk of 'selling out' at the same time as they were selling caricature on television and beyond.

Another potential commercial avenue was export. *Spitting Image* had a growing global reputation, winning international awards, such as third prize at the Rose d'Or competition in Montreux in May 1985, and International Emmys for Popular Arts in 1985 and 1986. It enjoyed (limited) export to the United States in 1985–6 and was packaged for sale to Western Europe. However, its major influence came in the various global remakes of the programme that appeared in the late 1980s and 1990s (Andrews, 2025). Programmes openly inspired by *Spitting Image* have been televised in France, Spain, Kenya, Israel, India, Argentina, Japan and South Africa, among others, but there is a variable degree of formality for these adaptations. While some, like Italy's *Teste di gomma* (TMC, 1987–8), were licensed versions on which members of the Spitting Image Productions team provided consultancy, most were unofficial borrowings. The best known of these, French *Les Guignols de l'info*, has itself inspired numerous global imitations.

While there have been informal international programme translations since the early days of television, it was not until the 1980s that 'content exchange' across borders began to cohere into the format business, developing by the 2000s into significant proportion of trade in the global television industry (Moran, 2013). *Spitting Image* appeared, then, at a moment in which the global trade in television formats was rapidly formalising and professionalising (Chalaby, 2016). However, as is by now familiar in this story, the selling of the programme internationally was piecemeal and ad hoc, somewhat different from the image of the TV format as a ruthlessly commercial response to market pressures that is often evoked in scholarship. In any case, copyright law is notoriously unfriendly both to television formats and to caricature, and the basic premise of 'puppet-based satirical sketch show' is too broad to be able to protect legally. Roger Law described his attempt to remake *Spitting Image* in Russia as 'not really a business proposition' (*Spitting in Russian*, 2010), and it is clear from archival evidence that this was a labour of love, or adventure, more than of profit generation. Indeed, many of the formatted versions of the show were made on significantly lower budgets than the UK original. For example, Law observed of the producer of Hungarian remake *Uborka* (Magyar Televízió, 1991–2002), 'he had a great deal of determination, but no money' (1997, 45). Therefore, while Spitting Image Productions was in a precarious financial position in the early 1990s, it was unable to use format sales to generate substantial additional funds.

The end, part I

In January 1990, William Sargent, CEO of visual effects firm The Frame Store (later Framestore), bought out Blair, Lloyd and Lambie-Nairn's shares in the company. He became Chairman of Spitting Image Productions, and took on its day-to-day management, with the stated aim of expanding its output. By November 1990, the company was, according to journalist John Dugdale, 'a more business-like, less pugnaciously radical organisation' (1990, 15). Several television programmes were developed, including *The Mary Whitehouse Experience* (BBC Two, 1991–2), an offshoot of a Radio 4 sketch show starring young comedians David Baddiel and Rob Newman (who were writers on *Spitting Image*), and *The Winjin' Pom* (ITV, 1991), a children's puppet show made using Spitting Image engineering, which cost £3m to make according to a *Times* report (Waller, 1990). Central was, by now, commissioning two series per year of the main programme. Taken together with merchandising, licensing and exhibitions that kept the programme in the public eye, the company gave the outward appearance of continuing success.

Things were not as they appeared to be. A January 1991 press release for the company strikes a downbeat tone. In it, Sargent is quoted saying '1991 will be as difficult for us as for everyone else in the industry' (Spitting Image Productions, 1991). Two factors converged to cause this doomsaying. The first was an economic downturn that led to a recession in 1990–1, depressing demand for advertising, while operating costs rose due to inflation. The second was changes to ITV's regulatory structure brought about by the 1990 Broadcasting Act. This legislation marked the culmination of the Conservative government's broadcasting policy developed through the 1980s, which applied its market-led economic approach to the TV industry. Margaret Thatcher viewed broadcasting as bloated and old-fashioned, in dire need of reform (Bonner and Aston, 1998, 360–2). To this end, a committee led by Alan Peacock met in 1985 to discuss the future of broadcast television in the UK. Peacock put 'consumer sovereignty' and the needs of the market at its centre of the enquiry, the first time a British broadcasting committee had not prioritised public service broadcasting (O'Malley and Jones, 2009). Putting some of Peacock's recommendations into action, the 1990 Broadcasting Act altered the composition and regulation of ITV. It required the broadcaster (alongside the BBC) to take 25 per cent of its programming from independent production companies. *Spitting Image* might have provided a superficial proof of concept for the ability of independents to deliver successful programmes, but it also demonstrated a persistent problem: the financial precarity caused by dependence on a limited number of commissions, and the inability to spread risk over a larger portfolio.

Spitting Image Ltd's planned expansion in the early 1990s was stymied both by the recession and by the uncertainty caused by the new system for determining who would run the regional ITV franchises. The Act disbanded the IBA, replacing it with a 'light touch' regulator, the Independent Television Commission (ITC). Its main function was to grant licences to run the ITV franchises, which were now to be awarded to the highest cash bid. The 1990 Award for Channel 3 (ITV) Licences shook up the system, where, according to Michael Darlow, a 'competent, well-reasoned but unimaginative' bid at auction could win over that of a 'bold imaginative and committed broadcaster' (2004, 535–6). As the system became more creatively conservative, it also put greater pressure on ITV programming to deliver viewers in a TV ecology where greater competition from cable and satellite was slowly but surely shrinking the available audience. With viewing figures averaging 6.5m an episode in 1994, *Spitting Image* no longer had the domestic commercial power it once had, and the ITC commented that 'the originality and wit of *Spitting Image* has declined' (Frean, 1996). Other projects, such as the Rubberworks and *The Winjin' Pom* did not generate anticipated revenue and Spitting Image Ltd struggled to balance its budgets. The final series aired in January and February 1996, with a later than usual 11.15 p.m. timeslot virtually guaranteeing a reduced audience.

Though the series had run its commercial and creative course, there were nevertheless repeated calls for the return of *Spitting Image*. Programmes with a similar premise of animated caricature appeared in various guises. Animated series *2DTV* (2001–4) was headed by *Spitting Image*'s last producers, Giles Pilbrow and Georgia Pritchett, who had also written for the show, and featured vocal talent from the series like Jon Culshaw and Jan Ravens. *Headcases* (2008) translated the caricature premise into computer-generated animation, where *Newzoids* (2015–16) combined live-action puppets with CGI. None of these series achieved the impact or longevity of *Spitting Image*, which meant that, even thirty years after its original broadcast, there remained a nostalgic demand for its return. This call would eventually be answered in a period of no less political or industrial turmoil than when the series first began: the year 2020.

Spitting Image rebooted

The British political environment of the late 2010s, deep in the shadow of a divisive referendum on the UK's membership of the European Union, was marked by populism, polarisation and growing public distrust in democratic institutions. Boris Johnson, Donald Trump and other global leaders maintained exaggerated public personas that lent them a strategic advantage in cutting through the noise of twenty-first-century politics and, as we saw in Chapter 2, made them eminently caricaturable. Stark divisions emerged between liberal and conservative attitudes, eroding consensus on moral standards which, in turn, left little agreement about the appropriate tone or subject matter for comedy, an intensification of the 'culture wars' that had been ongoing since the 1980s. In a reality that teetered perpetually on the edge of the absurd, the practice of caricature started to seem superfluous. Some commentators argued that satire was effectively 'dead', unnecessary or unable to exaggerate the vice and folly of contemporary politicians (Williams, 2016). These may seem inauspicious circumstances in which to launch a televisual caricature. For Roger Law (2022), though, the situation was reminiscent of the political scenario of the early 1980s, with populist governments led by strong personalities presiding over divided nations on both sides of the Atlantic. The time seemed right to bring back *Spitting Image*.

Law's original idea was to remake Alfred Jarry's *Ubu Roi* (1896), an absurdist parody of Shakespearean tragedy. Noting the similarities between the gluttonous, cruel, dishonest and vulgar protagonist and Donald Trump, he began to rewrite a satirical version, intending it for the theatre to avoid potential censorship (Law, 2022). He approached close friend Richard Bennett, who had managed the finances of Spitting Image Productions, for help. Both Bennett and former Managing Director Joanna Beresford now worked for Avalon, a transatlantic talent management, television production and live events company that specialised in comedy. A pilot was made in September 2019, intended for American audiences in a partnership between Avalon and a major US broadcaster. Some ideas from Law's *Ubu Roi* project were included, including a grotesque scene in which Trump's anus extends from his body to operate his smartphone while he sleeps. A year later, this sketch would be released on YouTube to promote

Fig. 3.5 Donald Trump discovers he has accidentally subscribed to Britbox, *Spitting Image* (2020)

the release of a *Spitting Image* reboot (Spitting Image, 2020). At the end of the video, Trump exclaims, 'Jesus Christ! The asshole's subscribed to Britbox!' (Fig. 3.5).

A bigger name than Britbox

Negative connotations of being the preferred streaming service of the president's rear end aside, this and other promotional videos jump-started the public association between *Spitting Image* and Britbox. For a second time, the show became flagship content intended to enhance the public image of a television provider, though in vastly different industrial circumstances than the 1980s. *Spitting Image* was the first original commission for Britbox UK, a joint venture between ITV (the majority owner) and BBC Studios. Britbox was envisioned as a British response to the 'streaming wars', a media-generated expression for the intense competition for consumers and content in the era of 'Peak TV'. This was prompted by the industry's move towards the 'subscriber model for cultural production', Amanda D. Lotz's (2017, 39–40) term for the economic arrangement by which consumers pay a recurring fee to access a collection of cultural goods curated by a provider that either funds the creation of new content or licenses it from other rights holders. This was adopted first in the US market, where high levels of conglomeration, vertical and horizontal integration created a small number of corporations with the large, cross-media content libraries needed to fuel the content-hungry subscriber model (Lotz et al., 2021, 277–8). Netflix, which became the globally dominant streamer, is an outlier, building a business model initially via licensing large volumes of third-party content for a relatively small subscription fee, and later moving into commissioning original content. Its move into the UK market, in 2012, accelerated consumer demand for box-set style video on demand (VOD) delivery, in contrast to the 'catch up' model that British broadcasters had developed since 2006 (Michalis, 2022). It was clear that the UK's long-established broadcasters would need new strategies to help them to compete.

Britbox (International), jointly owned by ITV and BBC Studios, launched in 2017 as a one-stop-shop for British TV and film, serving, initially, the North American market. Alexa Scarlata and Andrew Lynch (2023, 95) describe it as a 'second tier SVOD [subscription video on demand service]', an 'offshoot[] or subsidiar[y] of larger corporation with major media interests' that works by 'aggregating non-exclusive content or exploiting dust-gathering back catalogues owned by a parent company' (2023, 97). Second-tier status enables the service to avoid direct competition with the major streamers by serving a niche audience of Anglophiles. It entered the British market in 2019, with a different content library and operating structure than the international business. At its launch, Chief Executive Reemah Sakaan promised it would bring British viewers the 'faces, people and places that you know' (BBC News, 2019b). *Spitting Image* fulfilled this pledge not only by offering caricatures of well-known faces, but by associating Britbox with a high-profile, recognisable television brand. Reboots have been adopted more broadly in the age of 'Peak TV', a strategy with the economic benefits of reducing the risk of original commissions by attracting a presold, already-familiar audience, and the emotional advantages of nostalgia, with audiences and producers keen to revisit content enjoyed in their youth (Osur, 2022, 21–2). As Law (2022) put it, *Spitting Image* was 'a bigger name than Britbox'. Britbox had, indeed, struggled with brand recognition. Media consultants Oliver and Ohlbaum (2020) reported in March 2020 that more than a quarter of survey respondents had not heard of it, with a further 67 per cent having only tentative awareness of the streaming service. *Spitting Image* was high-impact programming capable of generating media interest, and therefore publicity, for Britbox. Echoing Denton's comments about commissioning the series for Central, Sakaan stated that Britbox 'wanted something noisy and brand defining that would grab people's attention' (Sweney, 2020). In this, it had the appearance of success: an ITV press release announcing the second series (only one week after the release of the first episode, in October 2020), claimed that the show had increased new subscribers to the platform 'tenfold' in the 24 hours after the show's launch (ITV Press Office, 2020).

Spitting Image is unusual as original content for an SVOD. Streaming services have tended to commission drama, feature film, documentary and some reality formats. Comedy originals have generally been sitcom (animated or live action) and stand-up. Satirical or political comedy has rarely been prioritised, with notable exceptions such as *Patriot Act With Hasan Minhaj* (Netflix) or *The Problem With Jon Stewart* (Apple TV+) (Andrews and Frame, 2025). This is because SVODs operate a non-linear provision model which better suits content that is not time sensitive. Because caricature is linked to the topical here-and-now, *Spitting Image* is temporally specific. With its focus on the comic minutiae of British politics and popular culture, it is also local. In other words, unlike most content for SVODs, it has the strong potential to suffer both temporal and cultural discounts (Hoskins, McFadyen and Finn, 2004, 48), the reduction in economic value accorded to media content the further it travels in time and space from its origins.

A British take on global events

Avalon's website describes *Spitting Image* as 'a uniquely British satirical take on global events', which neatly captures the show's contradictory aim to be both distinctively culturally British in its sense of humour and international in its outlook (Avalon, undated). Jeff Westbrook, who had written for *The Simpsons* (Fox, 1989–) and *Futurama* (Fox/Comedy Central/Hulu, 1999–), was recruited as showrunner to bolster the show's chances in the US market. He led a team that combined US and UK writing and vocal talent. Production meetings took place via videoconferencing, to overcome the limitations of both geography and COVID-19 lockdowns (Royal Television Society, 2021; Law, 2022). Cultural divergences exist in the standard method for writing comedy in the US and the UK. The US-centred 'writers' room', in which creative collaboration takes place to generate scripts, contrasts with the UK's more authored style, where individuals (or writing partnerships) craft scenes independently, which are later brought together by script editors or producers. Writer Matt Forde described the development of *Spitting Image* as a combination of these, with some sketches produced by individuals, some collaboratively in a (virtual) writers' room, and others edited in writing teams (Royal Television Society, 2021).

The sketch-writing style generated by these models also differs, with the US-based teams creating longer, more elaborate scenes, as opposed to the UK preference for shorter jokes. An example of a recurring sketch series centres on tech-billionaires Elon Musk, Jeff Bezos and Richard Branson, as they engage in a space race (Fig. 3.6). This satirises the ego-driven one-upmanship of the billionaires, alongside humorous critiques of their monopolistic empires and faulty goods and services (such as Amazon Prime, which fails to help Bezos conquer Mars quicker than his rivals despite its supposed 'expedited delivery'). These scenes were largely authored by US writers and have a mean average length of 1m 22 seconds, longer than the reboot's average sketch length of 1m 2 seconds (and indeed, the original series, which had

Fig. 3.6 Jeff Bezos, Elon Musk and Richard Branson engage in a new space race, *Spitting Image* (2020)

an average length of 55 seconds for its sketches). They have an ongoing story in the sitcom style that was trialled, and rejected, by the makers of the original series. Despite the cultural proximity of the US and UK, distinctions in the national sense of humour, especially in the tolerance for the crueller side of caricature, presented challenges to the production. Writing satire for an unfamiliar political culture also requires contextual knowledge, such that Westbrook depended on the UK writing team to provide a precis on British politics that would allow him to understand their sketches (Royal Television Society, 2021). Jokes that require explanations are notoriously antithetical to the success of comedy.

Targeting the US market was part of the plans for the remake from the very beginning of the reboot. The ambition was to partner with a major network on a US-centric *Spitting Image*, which would combine selected sketches from the British show with internationally salient figures (like Boris Johnson or Greta Thunberg) with extra scenes for American viewers. Avalon CEO Jon Thoday revealed in *The Times* that a deal was on the table with NBC until only weeks before the show premiered. He blamed the demise of the deal on the broadcaster's 'nervousness' that series may offend the Trump administration and its supporters

(Moore, 2020). History was apparently repeating itself. *Spitting Image*'s attempted launch into the US in 1986 ended when NBC chose not to option the series after it broadcast four specials that were critically acclaimed but achieved mediocre ratings (Andrews, 2025). Lloyd (2022) recalled that, at this time, an NBC executive had signalled interest in commissioning more, only to contact him a few days later to tell him they would not be continuing with the series. In the interim, the company had been bought out by General Electric, and executives were uneasy about the possibility that the show could be perceived as 'anti-American'. Similar sentiments were voiced in relation to NBC pulling out of the reboot: media correspondent Matthew Moore (2020) speculated that fears that the 'show's raucously insulting British humour … would not play well with an American family audience'. *Spitting Image* instead premiered on Facebook in the US. North American viewers would continue to access the series largely via social media clips.

While 'breaking America' had always been part of the ambitions for *Spitting Image*, the explicit focus on international audiences for the reboot demonstrates the TV industry's reorientation away from nationally specific content. This can partly be explained by economic factors in the era of 'Peak TV'. The need for attractive content libraries to sustain the 'subscriber model' has led to increased costs for television production. National broadcasters, especially PSBs, are less able than global conglomerates to finance these productions on their own, which has increased reliance on international finance. A return on investment is likelier for content that will sell across multiple territories and platforms. In any case, UK consumers have shown willingness to subscribe to services with minimal British content, which implies weak demand for nationally specific material, with the important caveat that there also is a substantive supply of broadcast video on demand (BVOD) services that caters to this market (Lotz and Eklund, 2024, 137–8). Taken together, this has caused 'concerns that UK broadcasters will over-focus on productions designed to sell well in international markets at the expense of United Kingdom-focused content with little wider export value' (Lotz et al., 2021, 281). Though SVOD services have invested in local content, original material that is able to travel is more favourable than highly specific material. Mareike Jenner (2018, 227–31) describes how Netflix originals, regardless of nation of origin, have adopted a 'grammar of transnationalism', manifested in the genres, aesthetics and value systems displayed in the programming. Content that is so culturally specific as to make it untranslatable is unappealing for SVODs. As outlined in Chapter 2, televisual caricature requires of its viewer a level of cultural competence, both in terms of the local knowledge of people and events that will aid distorted recognition, and of the standard, tone and appropriate subjects for humour. It defies this 'grammar of transnationalism', and is often untranslatable, making it a hard sell for global audiences.

Woke caricature?

The *Spitting Image* reboot emerged in an industry whose economic, technological and regulatory infrastructure was virtually unrecognisable from the context in which the original was made. Considering one such change, that of standards of governance, commissioning editor for Britbox Nana Hughes suggested that in the 1980s, 'compliance didn't exist, they just went for it and apologised afterwards: we can't do that' (Royal Television Society, 2021).[5] As we have seen, the original Spitting Image Productions team were not quite as cavalier as this implies, and maintained cordial working relationships with the IBA, negotiating to enable the broadcast of controversial material. Hughes's statement suggests a greater level of caution among television institutions in the 2020s, under the watch of Ofcom, than there had been in the 1980s. This goes beyond regulatory structures,

---

[5] Compliance is the vetting of content to ensure that it meets broadcasting and legal standards.

to more fundamental changes in cultural politics. Hughes argued that 'the things we could get away with in the 80s and 90s we certainly can't get away with now, and I didn't want to come in as the woke police' (Royal Television Society, 2021). It is noteworthy that Hughes, one of very few Black women to have worked on *Spitting Image*, should seek to avoid becoming associated with the putative self-censorship involved in contemporary comedy production. She connects the need for compliance with a broader arena of political division that has come to prominence in the past decade: the disputed terrain of social justice activism that has come to be known as 'woke'.

'Woke' originated in African American slang in the 1930s, to mean alertness to the threat of racism. It entered popular discourse in the 2010s in association with the Black Lives Matter (BLM) campaign and came to signify the consciousness of racial oppression (Kanai and Gill, 2021). It later broadened to incorporate awareness of other forms of oppression as well as to signal anti-racism. The association of wokeness with a 'liberal elite' has led to its demonisation in the UK by a nexus of right-wing commentators, politicians and media figures (Davies and MacRae, 2023). Discursively 'othering' those engaged in progressive causes, this group constructs 'wokeness' as an extremist position, taken up by a censorious 'mob' that seeks to deny 'the people' (implicitly framed as white Britons) the right to free speech. As with previous conservative backlashes against feminism, civil rights movements and so-called political correctness, 'woke' is positioned in this discourse as illegitimate, oversensitive and humourless. It is therefore framed as antithetical to comedy, as Bart Cammaerts explains:

> In the 'anti-woke culture war' discourse, freedom of speech to be racist and discriminatory is thus coupled with a divine freedom and right to offend others ... As the argument goes, 'nowadays you cannot say anything any longer, you're not allowed to laugh at anything, whereas in the good old days we could be unashamedly racist, sexist and/or homophobic ... how awful'. (2022, 739)

At the same time, from the mid 2010s, 'anti-woke' commentators began to vocally decry politically themed comedy that criticised the Conservative government, especially its Brexit policies, citing it as evidence of liberal bias and the 'woke agenda' operating through television (Andrews and Frame, 2025). Chapter 4 will explore in more detail the relationship between televisual caricature, offence and contemporary discourses of social justice. The 'culture war' related to 'woke', though, encompassed the specific 'conjuncture' in which the reboot was produced, distributed and received (Kanai and Gill, 2021).

Spitting Image occupied an ambivalent position in this context. Its comic modus operandi was to provoke, to be rude and indelicate, which required it to have a degree of licence to offend. That it would push the boundaries of acceptability was the key expectation that the *Spitting Image* brand established for its audience. But it was also made within an industry with the commercial incentive, and political, social and regulatory obligations, to pay attention to representation, on and off screen. The series had the contradictory task of living up to its reputation for offence, while avoiding alienating potential audiences (and customers for Britbox). During pre-production, ITV director Kevin Lygo met with the production team to discuss the need for cultural sensitivity and awareness in depictions of Black characters, in the light of the Black Lives Matter campaign (Yeates, 2020). Even before its release, promotional images of the puppets generated controversy. The design for the caricature of Mark Zuckerberg was criticised as drawing on Jewish stereotypes by the Campaign Against Antisemitism (Scully, 2020), while the choice to caricature environmental campaigner Greta Thunberg, who is autistic, was decried as insensitive and 'punching down' (Kemp, 2020). Whereas in the 1980s, most of the negative response to *Spitting Image* arrived in the form of conservative anxiety about the taste of its depictions of institutions (especially the royal family) and impact on the reputations of individuals, most of the pre-release concern about the reboot came from progressive voices. Law, no stranger to *Spitting Image* controversy, responded by critiquing those 'looking for things to complain about' and defended the caricatures on the basis that they were personal parody (Wilson, 2020). While Westbrook denied that any topic or individual was 'out of bounds' for the series, he did outline the intention to approach material in a 'thoughtful' way, employing caricature for its purpose of ridiculing its subjects' 'attitudes, arrogance, complacency or self-importance' (Hodges, 2021). As in the original series, the caricature function of the puppets was invoked to defend it against controversy, even if the critique tended to come from the opposite political persuasion than in the past. In this case, caricature's contradictions render it rhetorically capacious.

Perhaps unsurprisingly, 'woke' culture was mined as satirical subject matter for the *Spitting Image* reboot, across several sketches where the concept and its proponents are caricatured. In the first episode, for example, Lewis Hamilton, seated in his diesel-guzzling luxury car, positions himself as an advocate for social justice and environmental causes, a role that contradicts his sponsorship deals and tax arrangements. In the same episode, caricatured Disney executives attempt to cynically cash in on the popularity of Black Lives Matter by producing a Black Baby Yoda toy. Both sketches satirise the hypocritical adoption of 'woke' causes by privileged individuals or for corporate promotional purposes (Sobande, Kanai and Zeng, 2022). A more pointed satire on 'wokeness' comes in a sketch in which Boris Johnson absconds from parliament to join students who are isolated in their halls during the COVID-19 lockdowns (Fig. 3.7). He is disappointed to find that rather than the sex- and drug-fuelled parties he is anticipating, these 'woke' students are serious about their courses, determined to set rather than cross boundaries, critique his marijuana use as 'cultural appropriation' and spend their spare time 'curating a webpage for vegan profiteroles'. While the explicit subject of the caricature is Johnson, and his irresponsible evasion of duty and self-indulgent hedonism, the joke is *really* on 'woke'.

A comparison between the both the caricatured representations and personnel of the original and reboot of *Spitting Image* shows some interesting gaps between the reality and the

Fig. 3.7 Boris Johnson struggles to integrate with 'woke' students, *Spitting Image* (2020)

perception of the latter's 'woke' credentials. The overwhelming majority of puppets that appeared in the original series depicted white figures, 96 per cent of puppets used in series one to twelve. In nineteen episodes (around a fifth of the total), no puppets caricaturing people from racialised minorities appear at all. As previously noted, there was a huge imbalance in gender representation, with an average of only 18 per cent of total puppet appearances depicting female figures – and this figure is distorted by the prominence of Margaret Thatcher. Increases in the diversity of caricature representations for the reboot are noticeable, though the show is still dominated by white (70 per cent) and male (77 per cent) figures. These rather limited changes were also reflected in representation offscreen. In the writing team, the gender balance moved from 98 per cent male in the first twelve series, to a split of 82 per cent men and 18 per cent women in 2020, and 63 to 37 per cent for the final series.[6] A more significant shift occurred in

---

[6] Data about series personnel refer only to credited writers and performers. Identity data are best estimates based on available information. It is not possible to claim certainty in data about the gender or cultural identity of all individuals. For example, one of the female-coded credited writers on the second,

terms of cultural diversity. Where the writing team for the original series was almost exclusively white, 25 per cent of the writers on the reboot were from racialised minorities. ITV required a cultural match between voice actor and caricature subject, which resulted in a more diverse team of performers than in the original series. There are no performers from racialised minorities credited as acting talent in the original run of *Spitting Image*, which meant that the voices of Black characters, such as Robert Mugabe, Winnie Mandela, Frank Bruno or Trevor McDonald, were provided by white voice artists. By contrast, seven of the nineteen voice artists working on the reboot were people of colour. That such modest gains in the diversity of on- and off-screen representation were critiqued as indicative of the reboot's 'woke' credentials speaks to the polarisation of the 'culture wars' conjuncture (McPhee, 2021).

The question of 'woke' informed most reviews, and divisions along left/right lines were visible. Critics in right-wing papers accused *Spitting Image* of 'political correctness'/'wokeness' or 'pulled punches', and bias against Conservative figures (Moir, 2020; Singh, 2020; Delingpole, 2020). Critics in left-leaning outlets agreed that the series was 'toothless' (Wall, 2020). Arguing for the need for biting satire in the context of the 2020s, Nesrine Malik (2020) viewed *Spitting Image* as 'safe, purposeless and entirely unsuited to the political moment'. Even positive assessments of the show noted the context of 'sensitivity to offence' enhanced the risk of satirical television being 'policed by social media' (Lawson, 2020). Three other common strands appeared in critical reactions to the reboot, both among professional reviewers and on social media. The first was to reflect that, in a 24-hour news cycle, events move too quickly to be effectively satirised by television, and that social media made possible more responsive, immediate political comedy (Malik, 2020;

---

third and fourth series of *Spitting Image* was a pseudonym used by a male writer while freelancing on the show (Chester, 1986, 119). It has not been possible to source accurate credits for series 13–18.

Singh, 2020; Lawson, 2020). The second, to note that political actors as excessive and self-parodying as Boris Johnson and Donald Trump render caricature redundant (Maxwell, 2020; Reade, 2020). Finally, some critics suggested that while the puppets were visually effective and humorous, they are let down by weak writing (Moir, 2020; O'Grady, 2020). These echoed a persistent critical trend in relation to *Spitting Image*: in the words of one reviewer, ''Twas ever thus' (O'Grady, 2020).

The end, part II

The end of *Spitting Image* contained within it a curious echo of its beginning. In 1984, *Spitting Image* almost failed to make it to air because of a censorship row centred on the British royal family. Almost forty years later, the series was withdrawn from view because of the death of Queen Elizabeth II. ITV's 2022 Annual Report states that 'the business has written off the remaining Spitting Image episodes featuring the Queen, as they could not be effectively edited and so it is highly unlikely they will ever be screened' (ITV PLC, 2023, 61). The cost of this decision was reported at £9m (Bedigan, 2023). The statement misleadingly implies that new episodes of the series produced in 2022 had been withdrawn from schedules. In fact, the entire series (original and reboot) was quietly removed from Britbox's catalogue in the weeks after the Queen's death in September 2022. By late October, the cancellation of *Spitting Image* was reported in the press. A statement from Britbox linked this not to concerns about royal caricature, but to the cost of the show and to the forthcoming launch of ITV's new streaming service ITVX, into which Britbox was incorporated (Anderson, 2022). Taken together, these factors suggest that the *Spitting Image* reboot had been a rather costly failure.

Several factors worked against the reboot's success. The foremost was cost. Of itself, this is not an impediment to success in the arena of content production for SVODs. Rather, the opposite is true: most SVOD original programmes and films are expensive loss leaders, commissioned to provide an impactful, visible selling point to entice subscriptions. *Spitting Image* fulfilled this criterion as the 'noisy' content that Britbox desired. However, this did not translate into the number of new subscriptions needed to accrue substantial revenue, and Britbox made a venture loss for ITV of £59m in 2020 (ITV PLC, 2021, 13) and £61m in 2021(ITV PLC, 2022, 44). The first season was celebrated for generating a tenfold increase in new subscriptions, and ITV's 2021 Annual Report claimed 'steady growth' in subscribers, up to 733,000 by the end of the year (ITV PLC, 2022, 44). However, the falls significantly short of competitor SVODs in the UK: Netflix had 60 per cent penetration – around 17m households – by 2022, with Amazon Prime at 47 per cent and Disney+ at 23 per cent (Ofcom, 2022, 15). By the time the ITVX launched in December 2022, Britbox was no longer commissioning original content, including *Spitting Image*.

For the reboot to achieve similar levels of cultural ubiquity to the original, it would need to be seen by large numbers of people. This was constrained by its position as content for Britbox. A telling distinction between the impact of on-demand and broadcast viewing is that, where Britbox had fewer than half a million subscribers, the Election Special broadcast on ITV in November 2020 to provide a 'shop window' for the series, achieved viewing figures of 4.2m (BARB, undated a). This broadcast was not the only free to view preview of the show: a press release from Avalon cites over 200m global views for *Spitting Image* content online, shared across multiple social media and video platforms (Avalon, 2021). While this does demonstrate a significant level of international engagement with *Spitting Image*, it pales in comparison to other content produced by SVODs with global audiences, or indeed with social media content made on much smaller budgets.

Televisual caricature is subject to both the cultural and temporal discount, the fact that it is locally specific and topical. This renders it ineffective as long-term content for a non-linear platform. Where serial narrative fiction, the dominant form for SVOD flagship content, suits 'box set' viewing, binge-watching and 'on-demand' audience paradigms, the sketch-show format works better in more immediate medial contexts, broadcast or online. Content from this genre can be easily disaggregated and shared via social media both to promote it and generate fan engagement. The social media team for *Spitting Image* were adept at selecting sketches from the series relevant to current events as a means of generating interest. However, a strong social media presence is no longer optional, and is, in TV and comedy alike, an 'industry imperative' (Krefting and Baruc, 2015). Distributed on a traditional, televisual weekly release model, *Spitting Image* also suffered by comparison with the immediacy of satire on social media platforms. Because political comedy spreads rapidly via social media in response to current events, and jokes circulate, are adapted and appropriated by numerous users, the humour of *Spitting Image* could appear dated even when produced within a few hours of an event. It is difficult for television to respond comically to a news cycle as rapid as it was in 2020 and 2021. *Spitting Image*'s role and purpose was diminished in a context where 'humour as a widespread political communication device emerges as *not unique* to the internet but distinctly *of* the internet' (Davis et al., 2018, 3899).

True to the resilience shown through its long life, the cancellation by Britbox was not the end of *Spitting Image*. On 20 December 2021, as the second series was ending, Avalon announced plans for a live stage show. Titled 'Spitting Image Live featuring The Liar King', the poster pastiched the promotional image for long-running West End musical *The Lion King*, with the puppet version of Boris Johnson's head bursting through its centre. This announcement predated the removal of Johnson from office by six months, but the prime minister had already developed a strong reputation for his economy with the truth. Plans for the show were well underway during the first part of 2022 for puppet-centred musical based loosely on Johnson's story in a spoof of *The Lion King* (Law, 2022). By July 2022, Johnson had resigned as prime minister in the wake of multiple scandals. A reconfigured version of the show centred on the royal family had to be adapted again after the Queen's death (Newman, 2023). The show was finally staged in 2023, first at the Birmingham Rep Theatre in February and March, and then the Phoenix Theatre in London's West End, from May to August.

Titled *Idiots Assemble*, the musical loosely parodies superhero movies, with a plot involving a crack international team, led by a tiny Tom Cruise puppet, dispatched by King Charles III to vanquish a malevolent cabal of powerful antagonists including Johnson, Trump, Elon Musk and Rupert Murdoch. While on-stage puppeteers manipulated the characters, voices were delivered through the PA system. Additional lines of dialogue were recorded regularly to maintain a level of topicality. In the performance I attended, recent events such as the then Home Secretary, Suella Braverman's emerging policy of deporting refugees to Rwanda, transport strikes and a 'cost of living crisis' were woven into the script.[7] Elements of the original conception of The Liar King are still traceable in the final show, with parody versions of 'The Circle of Life' and 'I Just Can't Wait to Be King' sung by Tory leadership candidates. Other West End Musicals, such as *We Will Rock You* are referenced, as are aspects of the original series, such as a rendition of 'Tomorrow Belongs to Me' from *Cabaret*, used to chilling and memorable effect in the 1987 Election Special. This suggests the anticipated audience is old enough to be familiar with the original *Spitting Image*. The show addresses the question of 'woke' head on in an opening voiceover monologue which announced a 'trigger warning', that the show would 'respect no ideologies or religions' and directs audience members to 'leave if you are a humourless prick'. As in Law's original conception for the reboot of using the theatre to circumvent censorship, this promised a show that might offend delicate sensibilities. While some of the caricatures (especially Braverman, portrayed as a psychotic ghoul) were personally insulting to

---

[7] I attended the matinee performance of the West End run on 1 June 2023. The show was still in previews.

the subject, the show, like the series, tiptoed through a political middle ground, prodding rather than skewering targets left and right.

Conclusion

By adapting *Spitting Image* from screen to stage, *Idiots Assemble* provided a reminder of the materiality of the puppets and their origin as three-dimensional models. While television provided the most visible and effective vehicle for these caricatures, they have always had a life beyond it. As Law noted, 'If *Spitting Image* shows have achieved anything, they took the political cartoon from print into another medium, television' (Royal Television Society, 2021). In exploring this case study, certain conclusions can be drawn about the place of televisual caricature in the highly changeable industry that makes it. The first is to consider what made *Spitting Image* an attractive proposition to commissioners at Central in 1983 and to Britbox in 2020. Both sought 'noisy' content that would capture attention and contribute to (re)constructing their brand image. Televisual caricature is in a uniquely advantageous position to do this because it appropriates pre-existing interest in its famous subjects. It offers the distinctive pleasure of distorted recognition, of seeing familiar faces made ridiculous in a humorous clash of reality and fantasy. As an extension of the British satirical tradition, it can be positioned (by producers, broadcasters and regulators) as a legitimate critique, even defended as performing a moral duty and serving the public interest by holding those in power to account.

Drawing on the traditions of satire, televisual caricature is tied by its referentiality to a specific time and place. In the 1980s and 1990s, *Spitting Image* exploited the immediacy associated with broadcast television to appear highly topical, even though the intense production schedule for the show limited the amount of truly recent material to a few minutes per episode. For Central, this was of strategic advantage, creating a 'watercooler' effect that kept the show in the public consciousness. Although caricatures of international figures featured prominently in the series, its sense of humour, and most of its targets, were British. The volume of remakes of *Spitting Image* (as opposed to direct export of the show) suggests that televisual caricature has more resonance and viability when it is tailored for local audiences. In an industry that was, in the 1980s and 1990s, largely delimited nationally, this is no impediment. For the reboot, though, the temporal and local specificity of televisual caricature proved to be a disadvantage. The ideal qualities for television content have shifted alongside the dominant distribution method (put simply, from broadcast to on-demand). Where topical content may have previously had an audience-gathering function, it is now a liability in an industry that prioritises content to be accessed at any time.

The strategic use of televisual caricature as impactful content is not without risk. The cruelty of caricature, in its grotesque deformation of the individual, lends it an ever-present potential to offend. Even before the programme aired, its commissioner and the regulator recognised the likelihood that *Spitting Image* would cause controversy among certain sectors of the audience and the press. Censure for the series came largely in the shape of conservative backlash against its portrayal of institutions, especially the royal family. Regardless of how gentle the caricature was, the royals were considered unable to defend themselves and therefore inappropriate subjects for satire. Initial disagreements between Spitting Image Productions, Central and the IBA about the boundaries within which the show must stay subsided into a gentlemanly understanding that stopped short of censorship. Little critical attention was paid to the stereotypical elements of the caricatures, nor to the absence of women and especially people of racialised minorities in its depiction of the public realm. By 2020, the direction of travel for offence was two-way. From the left, progressive voices were quick to critique caricature that drew too heavily on stereotype or (in an echo of attitudes to the royals) seemed to traduce individuals felt not to 'deserve' such treatment. From the right, proponents of the 'anti-woke culture war' appeared actively to desire hurtful caricatures of figures to whom they were opposed. From both sides, the show was criticised for pulling its punches. Televisual caricature may be most effective as content in a divided political culture, but these circumstances also render audiences more difficult to please.

The knotty arguments about the political status of televisual caricature manifested in debates about the permissible limits of offence in relation to *Spitting Image*. There is a political and moral case to be heard about the acceptability of televisual caricature. Is it justifiable to use a highly visible public platform like television to ridicule an individual? What redress is available to its targets? And how can we best respond to some televisual caricature's employment of undesirable representational practices such as stereotyping or blackface? Chapter 4 will explore these arguments in relation to the 'culture war' debates that have been touched on in this chapter, considering how televisual caricatures from the 1990s and 2000s were reappraised in the light of events in 2020.

4

Cancelling Televisual Caricature

Introduction

The last chapter examined how *Spitting Image*'s reboot was stymied, in part, by the divided political culture of the time of its release and the perception that it was 'too woke' to be effective caricature. This chapter takes seriously the idea that televisual caricature is incompatible with social justice. Thorny ethical questions about who gets to joke about whom are key to the cultural politics of comedy. For televisual caricature, the extra dimension of imitation is added to this conundrum, so the question becomes 'who is permitted to comically impersonate whom?' A particularly problematic example is blackface performance, where make-up, wigs and other prosthetics are used to alter the appearance of a performer to mimic the skin tone, hair and other features associated with a different racialised group to their own.[1] Blackface minstrelsy has a long history in North America, and was successfully exported to the UK, where it enjoyed theatrical and, thanks to long-running variety programme *The Black and White Minstrel Show* (BBC One, 1958–78), televisual prominence throughout the twentieth century (Pickering, 2008; Johnson, 2012; Grandy, 2020; A. Thompson, 2021). In what follows, I analyse blackface

---

[1] This applies in most cases, though 'blackface' can also describe caricatured impersonations (often but by no means always satirical or parodic) by Black performers.

televisual caricatures and their legacies. I write as a white British woman who has not had first-hand experience of racism, but who has witnessed the effects of racist discrimination, exclusion and bias, and the backlash against their being made more socially, culturally and politically visible.

As its title suggests, the chapter considers what it might mean for televisual caricature to be 'cancelled'. Eve Ng (2022) describes a variety of 'cancel practices' that have emerged in recent years, including admonishment for the transgression of socially acceptable norms, boycotts of corporations, institutions or individuals as a material punishment for improper behaviour or actions and, at the extreme end, attempts to remove the person and/or their work from public life. Blackface televisual caricature became an object of public cancellation at a specific moment in time, June 2020. The murder of George Floyd, a Black man from Minneapolis, Minnesota, who died after white police officer Derek Chauvin compressed his neck for nine minutes, became a global media event after damning video evidence of the brutal act circulated on social media. The Black Lives Matter (BLM) movement and its calls for social justice for Black people (in the United States and elsewhere in the West) received heightened attention. This in turn led to widespread recriminations and/or public expressions of regret for past instances of racist attitude or behaviour amongst a range of famous individuals and institutions, often couched in terms of 'doing better' or 'listening and learning'. Significant among these were the 'outing' of public personalities who had blacked up in their past, including Canadian Prime Minister Justin Trudeau and TV hosts Jimmy Kimmel and Jimmy Fallon, prompting a renewed interest in, and condemnation of, blackface (A. Thompson, 2021, 5–19). The television industry responded by issuing apologies and by removing instances of blackface performance in comedies from their public content archives (Herr, 2020). This chapter evaluates this event as a moment in television history, considering its implications for the cultural politics, industrial position and post-broadcast afterlife of televisual caricature.

I begin by surveying analytical approaches to blackface, looking at televisual caricature's place in debates about comedy, offence, racism and 'political correctness'. I go on to explore the legacy of specific instance of blackface caricature, the appearance of comedian David Baddiel as footballer Jason Lee in a sketch as part of the comedy chat show *Fantasy Football League* (BBC2 1994–6). This skit was part of an ongoing joke at Lee's expense that Baddiel and comedy partner Frank Skinner have subsequently conceded was racist, and amounted to bullying (Wollaston, 2022). I analyse this instance of blackface caricature, as well as responses to it from poet Marvin Thompson, caricature target Lee and Baddiel. Baddiel has himself been the target of an antisemitic televisual caricature, as part of the surreal sketch comedy *Bo Selecta* (Channel 4, 2002–4). A loose satire of early 2000s celebrity culture, *Bo Selecta*'s skits involved comedian Leigh Francis wearing poorly constructed facial masks and using deliberately inaccurate vocal impressions to create bizarre caricatures of celebrities, including several Black British and American stars. In June 2020, Francis issued an apology for his racist caricatures, and *Bo Selecta* was removed from Channel 4's digital streaming service (a de facto public archive). The chapter concludes with an evaluation of these attempts to rectify racist televisual caricature via an incomplete cancellation.

Blackface impersonation and racist (televisual) caricature

Ng (2022) describes 'cancel culture' as the combination of both 'cancel practices and 'cancel discourses', the commentary that accompanies them on social media platforms (first-order discourses) and legacy media such as broadcast television or journalism (second-order). 'Cancel discourse' includes the positing – from both conservatives and liberals – of cancellation as an excess of the left, one that threatens to limit free speech. 'Cancel culture' is an outgrowth of the so-called 'culture wars', a term widely used to refer to the erosion of political and moral consensus and broadening gap between liberal and conservative values. Jim McGuigan suggests that in the early 1990s the culture wars manifested in a 'new conservative dogmatism' against 'political correctness', though he also argues that, on the other side of the political spectrum 'a certain humourless and evangelical radicalism was indeed evident on many [university] campuses' (2002, 17). Note the equation of the progressive left with a deficiency of humour. This is a recurrent theme in debates about comedy, offence and political correctness. Those invested in social justice are imputed to be unable to take a joke, either through misplaced oversensitivity or through the lack of sophistication required to understand ironic discourse (Cammaerts, 2022). Political correctness is framed here as censorship, designed to suppress free expression and authentic discourse, replacing it with an artificial politeness that obscures deeper cultural anxieties. This is the inverse of the aims of caricature, which seeks to pull to the surface the 'truth' of its targets, to externalise what is latent or essential. Where caricatures use superficialities to reveal, political correctness – defined this way – uses them to conceal.

The field of humour ethics offers a range of responses to the disputed permissibility of 'politically incorrect' joking. Some scholars take the 'exculpatory approach' (Weaver, 2011, 8), the view that comic discourse should be exempt from normative moral assessments because it is a fundamentally unserious, playful form of speech: 'just jokes'. This perspective is most associated with sociologist Christie Davies, who argued that 'comedy is unimportant because it has no effect and no consequences at all in a world where social change is driven by other far stronger social forces' (2016, 35). The opposing view takes seriously the potential of humour to enact a moral or psychic violence. Michael Billig, for example, argues that 'there is a body of joking to which the appropriately moral response is not laughter, but outrage' (2005, 43). Indeed, as Raúl Pérez (2021, 21) argues, the insidious power of racist humour is to cloak its socially harmful effects in a form that is commonly viewed as harmless, even 'delightful'.

For many analysts of race and humour, context is crucial to determine the ethical suitability of joking. Context can refer to the broader sociopolitical culture in which joking takes place, the ideological frame in which the joke is situated, the identity of the joke-teller and joke-hearer, the subject matter of the comedy and who or what is the 'butt' of the joke. The ethical position of humour depends on who is telling jokes about whom, to whom and in what circumstances. Luvell Anderson (2023) seeks to distinguish racist jokes from 'merely racial' and 'racially insensitive' ones to avoid 'conceptual inflation', the expansion of concepts that broaden and dilute their meaning. His definitions depend on the positions of speaker and audience to the 'racially stratified social order', in other words, the uneven distribution of people across social categories organised by perceived racial identities. 'Merely racial' comedy occurs when a joker seeks to subvert this order and an audience can be reasonably expected to recognise that aim. 'Racially insensitive' joking happens when speakers aim to subvert the racially stratified social order but fail to attend to relevant contextual features. The term 'racist' is reserved for humour that aims to 'reinforce the hermeneutic resources' of or take place in a context that 'forecloses interpretations that challenge the racially stratified social order' (Anderson, 2023, 378). Analyses of racist humour have moved beyond the important practice of definition, to evaluate its effects. Pérez, for example, explores racist humour as a 'powerful mechanism for reinforcing boundaries of inclusion, exclusion and dehumanization' (2021, 18). He describes how 'amused racial contempt' perpetuates racist ideologies and white racial dominance by enabling a racism characterised not only by ignorance and hate but by 'pleasurable racial solidarity' (2021, 48). Such solidarity is enabled by racist humour's delineation between the 'outgroup' that it makes its subject, and the 'we' to whom the joke is addressed. Far from 'just jokes', racist humour both reflects and constructs the workings of social power, acting as 'propaganda in support of racist ideology' (Howitt and Owusu-Bempah, 2005, 49).

Blackface impersonation is the most relevant iteration of racist humour for the analysis of televisual caricature.

Ayanna Thompson (2021) traces the long theatrical history of blackface, distinguishing the broader tradition from its best known 'specific performance mode', blackface minstrelsy. Minstrelsy originated in early nineteenth-century North America, initially as a form of street performance which migrated into show-business contexts of circuses, variety houses and theatres (A. Johnson, 2021, 6). Pérez describes it as a 'ritualized form of racial ridicule' that played a role in 'forging and popularising notions of racial superiority and inferiority in early US society' (2021, 14). Blackface minstrelsy was exported to the UK as early as the 1830s and became a common feature of popular entertainment throughout the nineteenth century. Pickering (2008) argues that in its cultural export, boundaries were blurred between blackface minstrelsy in the US and UK, but distinctive British aspects emerged from early on in its history. He explains that part of the popular appeal of the minstrel show lay in 'temporally regulated admission of forms of character and feeling neither condoned nor cultivated as British' (2008, 185). This created a convenient distance that, as we will see, aided in the defence of blackface minstrelsy well into the twentieth century. Although the live minstrel show declined in popularity, it was translated into other media forms, including radio and, later, television (Pickering, 2008).

There are instances of black and brownface performance across British television history, for example, in race-centric sitcoms such as *Curry and Chips* (ITV, 1969) and *The Melting Pot* (BBC One, 1975), the latter of which was withdrawn from broadcast after only one episode (Duguid, undated).[2] But it was most visible in *The Black and White Minstrel Show*, a popular variety programme that was broadcast for twenty years on weekend evenings and described by the BBC as 'good hearted family entertainment' (*The Times*, 1967, 3). The programme consisted of a series of skits

---

[2] Brownface refers to the analogous practice of light-skinned performers using make-up to mimic people with darker complexion than their own, often to imitate South Asian, North African, Middle Eastern, Latin American or First Nations people.

and song and dance numbers, usually ragtime showtunes associated with the Southern states of the US, performed in a studio dressed to resemble the theatrical settings in which minstrel shows typically appeared. White performers' faces were painted to appear black, aside from the use of chalk-white paint around the eyes and lips, which are made grotesquely large through the make-up design. This is consistent with physiognomic exaggerations that appear repeatedly in caricature imagery of Black people, serving to construct what Rebecca Wanzo calls a 'visual grammar that always haunts attempts at full enfranchisement' (2020, 2). Its repetitive consistency makes blackface make up work as a 'mask', a 'single constant component, regardless of performer, persona, costume or setting, allowing them to be what, formally, they were not' (Pickering, 2008, 85–6). The 'mask' is central to minstrelsy's practice of racial impersonation, serving both to conceal the identity of the performer and reveal the racialised persona of the minstrel character. Impersonation, as explored in Chapter 2, entails the embodiment of a subject, via imitation of gesture, voice, mannerism and movement. In the *Black and White Minstrel Show* (and other forms of minstrelsy) this was not individuated impersonation of the kind explored throughout this book, but an imitation of a stock type developed from exaggerated appropriations that mock Black performance styles. 'Mock' operates here in Jonathan Greenberg's (2018) terms as both an attempt at mimesis *and* a form of ridicule (see Introduction), in common with (televisual) caricature. Intrinsic to minstrelsy, in *The Black and White Minstrel Show* and elsewhere, is the reiterative performance of racialised caricature.

The Black and White Minstrel Show's longevity and position in the BBC's peak time schedules may appear peculiar to contemporary observers. Its popularity, too, (with an audience reach of up to 16m viewers) can serve to obscure the controversy it engendered throughout much of its broadcast life (Hendy, 2022). It was, in fact, the subject of public resistance, which was met by institutional defence (even defensiveness) on the part of the BBC. Christine Grandy (2020) found that the BBC presented minstrelsy as an 'established custom' in the UK in response to accusations of racism, for example from the Campaign Against Racial Discrimination (CARD). It claimed that the show was 'not about race'. Grandy argues that rhetorically divorcing minstrelsy from racism was made possible by framing the imagined (white) audience for the show as 'colour-blind' or 'racially innocent' 'seemingly unable and unwilling to acknowledge racialized structures within forms of entertainment' (2020, 862). For Ayanna Thompson, such appeals to 'white innocence' invoke an 'inherent white supremacist logic' (2021, 18). A 1967 memo from a senior BBC officer makes the case that the series should not cause alarm because it was unlikely to 'contaminate' viewers who were not already racially prejudiced, a telling choice of words in the context of a defence that depended on infantilising assumptions about the (white) public's moral purity on racial matters. This officer also made the case that it is the protest, rather than the show itself, that is likely to inflame those who are racially prejudiced, concluding that Black people offended by the show, for their own sake, should 'shut up' (Hendy, 2022). The outcome of public campaigns like CARD identifying blackface performance as racist was to prick the bubble of 'white innocence', and to

> prompt[] outcries by white audiences and producers who denied or resented the authority of black and Asian immigrants to name British customs as problematic, and who denied their own central roles as a majority white audience catered to by a media that was itself highly dependent on the appeal of racialized screen content to audiences. (Grandy, 2020, 884)

This response is also familiar in the twenty-first century, where public calling out of acts of racism is often met with an oppositional reaction, where critics are accused of 'bringing race into everything'. Such defensive responses become implicated in a broader trend in the (cultural) public sphere that Gavan Titley describes as the 'debatability of racism', where 'the very mention of race serves as an invitation to disprove its salience, the mention of racism as an invitation to refute its relevance' (2019, 2).

'Racial innocence' defences of blackface on television substantially depended on an assumed familiarity with and tacit approval of minstrelsy as a 'custom' devoid of racial content. Another means by which it has been explained and/or justified is through appeals to historical ignorance. As we will see, performers who have been compelled to reappraise their past acts of blackface caricature have invoked ignorance of the 'custom', its origins and the harms it has caused. Philosopher Charles Mills has called this 'white epistemological ignorance', summarised by Pérez as a

> not knowing that allows whites to minimize knowledge of racial harm, render whiteness and racism invisible, and marginalize the history and memory of white racial domination and its impact on the present by putting white racism out of sight and out of mind. (2021, 37)

This can be exacerbated by the transnationalisation of blackface performance. Pickering (2008, 3–4) emphasises that, in the export of the minstrelsy tradition to the UK, blackface performance did not speak to a racialised sense of difference in Britain in the same way that it did in North America. Titley (2019, 56–65) analyses the mediated discourse around Zwarte Piet, a blackface caricature that has long featured in Dutch Christmas traditions (including television programming), finding similar discourses of innocence and custom to the defence of the *Black and White Minstrel Show*. Critics of Zwarte Piet pointed to blackface as a dehumanising practice and insisted on its connections to the Netherlands' history of colonialism and its ongoing resonance in the present. Defenders tried to discredit these arguments, pointing to the tradition of the blackface as 'merely' signifying coal dust, and refuting the practice's racism by disowning a connection to colonialism, while claiming the contemporary nation as 'postracial'. In these cases, white epistemological ignorance combines with colonial amnesia and denial.

Though not all instances of blackface performance are impersonations of a specific individual, there is nevertheless a strong overlap between blackface and caricature. Both involve a tension between distortion and mimesis, both exaggerate physical, especially physiognomic, features to aid recognition, and both entail superficial signification that requires a much broader set of cultural and social 'knowledges' (see Chapter 2). These are characteristics shared with stereotypes, which 'exaggerate and homogenise traits held to be characteristic of particular categories and serve as blanket generalisations for all individuals assigned to such categories' (Pickering, 2001, 10). Caricature and stereotype are both perceived as synonymous with representational dishonesty, act as semiotic shorthand and can communicate cultural consensus and shared understandings, however erroneous these may be. Though caricature and stereotype are often used interchangeably in everyday speech, my definition of televisual caricature, with its emphasis on individuation, distinguishes between them. Portrait caricature, designed to use distortions to aid recognition of an individual, pulls in the opposite direction to stereotype, which uses them to homogenise and reduce the individuality and humanity of their subject. As Wanzo notes, because caricature externalises human failings, follies and excesses, 'being portrayed as a caricature can be a sign of your humanity' (2020, 14). In their distortions, deformations and diminution of the humanity of their subjects, caricature and stereotype are both liable to cause harms. In its more general sense of exaggerated comic depiction, caricature has been used to visualise or spectacularise stereotype, in images that perpetuate discriminatory and oppressive attitudes and effects.

Patricia Hill Collins describes caricatures of Black women in the US as 'controlling images' which are 'designed to make racism, sexism, poverty and other forms of social injustice appear to be natural, normal and inevitable parts of everyday life' (2022, 91). 'Controlling images' create and perpetuate the status of Black women as 'Other', constructing ideological grounds on which their oppression is maintained. The use of caricature to ridicule

Africans and Black people has a long history in the English satirical tradition (Odumosu, 2017), while the ubiquitous circulation of caricature imagery of African people was part of the everyday visual culture of nineteenth-century Britain, one which helped to reinforce racist discourses used to justify colonialism (Pickering, 2001). Wanzo (2020, 4) describes this as 'visual imperialism', noting the historical concurrence of the rise of caricature as a popular representational form and biological racism in the mid-nineteenth century. One rationale for racist hierarchisation depended on the pseudoscience of physiognomy, the association of facial features with moral and personal characteristics. This assumption that a person's essence can be 'read' from their face, was also instrumental to the work of caricature in the nineteenth century (Gombrich and Kris, 1938). Wanzo argues that these dual histories mean that caricature therefore has ambivalent connotations in relation to Blackness, 'given the hypervisibility of racism in black representational histories' (2020, 13). Blackface minstrelsy can be included as part of this visual regime.

Given its implication in these histories, blackface has been the subject of moral analysis. Asking directly 'what's wrong with blackface?', Robin Zheng and Nils-Hennes Stear (2023) examine the ethical case. They argue that artworks 'prescribe' the adoption of certain attitudes in their viewer (see Chapter 2's discussion of 'address'). They can therefore have intrinsic moral properties, that is, how they express moral attitudes via these prescriptions, and extrinsic ethical flaws related to the consequences of exposure to them. The harm caused by caricature's perpetuation of racist ideologies is an extrinsic ethical flaw. But it is the intrinsic moral unacceptability of blackface that Zheng and Stear seek to establish. They distinguish between two kinds of prescription for artworks: 'endorsement', presenting an attitude as suitable for 'export' into the outside world, and 'fictive deployment', which requires the temporary suspension of some beliefs to 'play along' with attitudes without necessarily adopting them. Invoking Collins's 'controlling images' thesis, they establish that blackface minstrelsy's anti-Black history has 'profound implications for understanding why blackface almost always fictively deploys anti-Black attitudes' (2023, 396). On this basis, even where there is no clear intention to endorse racism prescribed by blackface performance, blackface fictively deploys anti-Black attitudes that realise and normalise oppression, and licence oppressive acts. Zheng and Stear hypothesise a kind of 'critical blackface' that could be deployed to critique anti-Black racism. For Amanda N. Brand, a satirical mode for blackface performance opens a 'discursive space in which stereotypes can be inverted, their morality questioned' (2023, 218). Brand compares this with two other 'humour ecologies' in which televised blackface has appeared: the 'weakly reflexive', which draws on stereotypes without endorsing them, but also without actively challenging the ideologies from which they emerge; and the racist, which 'unreflexively privileges Whiteness and subordinates Blackness' (2023, 221). For Brand, the moral acceptability of blackface performance depends upon the humour ecology in which it is situated. Nevertheless, in the case of the potentially subversive or anti-racist deployment of blackface, Zheng and Stear conclude that it is morally reckless given the high likelihood of failure and misunderstanding.

I perceive two problems with the invocation of 'satire' to justify blackface performance. First, defending blackface as 'satire' implies that those who may be offended by it lack the necessary sophistication to understand it. Offence is framed as an inappropriate response to blackface performance on the grounds of a deficiency of interpretation. In opposition to the 'racial innocence' defence of blackface (such as the case of *The Black and White Minstrel Show*), which assumes that a viewer who 'sees race' in blackface reads too much, to deny the offensiveness of blackface on the grounds of satire assumes that the injured party reads too little. For Anshuman Mondal (2018, 39), satire has acted as a 'moral alibi' that has provided a dubious 'free speech' justification for comic offence. Second, the dominant effect of satire on its target is a loss of dignity. In an argument largely focused on traditional satire's targets of people or institutions in power, Giselinde Kuipers (2015) argues that the potential outcome of this loss of dignity is a weakening of authority, a diminution of that power. She suggests, then, that the response to satire must mitigate its effects for the target to save face. She assesses several possible responses for satirical targets in relation to dignity. To ignore the satire can signify strength or weakness, depending on the relative social authority already enjoyed by the target. Laughing along can 'take the worst sting out of the satire', but this is easier the higher the social status of the target and must be done in a way that looks 'authentic'. There is also a risk in this case of implicitly endorsing the joke and the attitudes that it conveys. Joking back contains satire within a humorous frame but requires the target to have resources of power and access to the public sphere. Arguing against the satire to rebut it is logically and legally possible through, for example, defamation law, but is rarely successful and, in any case 'the juxtaposition of satire with serious objection flatters the satirist' and strongly implies the truth of the satire (2015, 28). To show anger, shame, embarrassment or withdrawal clearly have strong implications for the power status of the target, but can also for the satirist, since, as Kuipers argues, 'while it is amusing to see dignity attacked, it is less enjoyable to see dignity destroyed' (2015, 28). I will return to these potential responses for satirical targets when examining the impact of specific instances of racist televisual caricature. To employ blackface caricature in the service of satire is to engage in a representational form that fundamentally seeks to diminish the dignity of its subject. While the 'target' of satirical blackface may not be a Black person, or Black people, or Blackness as an identity, the performance mode in which the satire takes place is one which is predicated on racialised ridicule designed to denude its subject of dignity.

This survey of scholarship on the cultural politics of televisual caricature, blackface and the ethics of racist humour has served to sharpen a definition of racist televisual caricature. A caricature is racist when it is the target's cultural, ethnic or racial background that is being ridiculed, explicitly or implicitly, or when personal ridicule is filtered through the prism of race. Racist televisual caricature bases its ridicule not (only) on an individuated 'caricature signature' but on racialised or stereotypical tropes or features, or where the 'caricature signature' involves the imitation and exaggeration of vocal or bodily signifiers or gestures that are substantially associated culturally with a specific ethnic group. Racist televisual caricature causes harm beyond the personal affront that might be taken by the individual targeted. It matters because 'racist humour is a discourse that has long played, and continues to play, a powerful role in creating and maintaining racist feelings, hierarchies, and worldviews' (Pérez, 2021, 5). Televisual caricature's position as an artefact of the cultural public sphere enables it to contribute to the conditions that exclude certain groups from full and equal citizenship and participation in the public sphere. Whether or not it might be funny, whether its moral flaws are extrinsic or intrinsic, whether the humour ecologies in which it is embedded are racist, weakly reflexive or satirical, I find it to be indefensible. Nevertheless, it exists as a part of television history. We are obligated, then, to assess the cultural, social and personal consequences of blackface televisual caricature.

A pineapple on his head: The legacy of a blackface televisual caricature

On 25 March 2021, almost a year after the murder of George Floyd had spurred a global reckoning with the meaning and effects of structural, interpersonal and cultural racism, the UK's Poetry Society announced that the winner of its National Poetry Competition 2020 was Marvin Thompson's *The Fruit of the Spirit is Love (Galatians 5:22)*. The poem is a densely intertextual account of the experience of growing up Black in 1990s Britain, the subtle and overt racism experienced in that context, the regret at engaging in the racist ridicule of another Black person and the impact this might have on raising a new generation of mixed heritage children. Among allusions to the Bible, African American artists Billie Holiday, Wu-Tang Clan and Spike Lee, and a painting by Salvador Dalí, Thompson directly references an instance of blackface televisual caricature. One stanza reads,

> "... a pineapple on his head ..." sang football fans
> and a comedian blacked up as Jason Lee,
> mocking Rastas ...

In a video released by The Poetry Society, Marvin Thompson (2021) reads *The Fruit of the Spirit*, framed in the centre of the screen in medium closeup, directly addressing the camera. For this part of the poem, he breaks from reading and sings 'a pineapple on his head' to the tune of *He's Got the Whole World in His Hands*, repeating the refrain and forcing a break in the poem's metre. This creates a jarring moment of sudden and sinister levity, as Thompson raises his eyebrows, tilts his head slightly and widens his eyes to convey the taunting tone of the chant. This melody – an African American spiritual – provides another intertextual layer in the performed version of the poem, since the song is simultaneously invoked and distorted in an act of racial mockery. Thompson's reading of the next line places a questioning intonation on the words 'blacked up', his brow furrows and eyes narrow while meeting the gaze of the camera, conveying a sense of bewilderment, disbelief and hurt at the memory of this televisual caricature.

The 'skit' caricature referred to here (see Chapter 2) appeared in *Fantasy Football League*, a weekly football-themed chat show hosted by comedians David Baddiel and Frank Skinner. The programme's loose format involved Baddiel and Skinner bantering about the week's football with celebrity guests, interspersed with skits based on impersonations of football personalities. Baddiel has described these performances as 'cartoons', conveying their exaggeration, silliness and childishness, interestingly connoting caricature's effects without using the term (Wollaston, 2022). One skit begins with Nottingham Forest FC manager Frank Clark, played by Skinner, surveying a newspaper article about potential changes to goal size in professional football, then using an intercom to request a nameless PA 'send him in'.[3] 'Him' is Jason Lee, played by Baddiel. He appears from behind a door,

---

[3] This episode aired BBC2, 12 January 1996, 23.15.

dressed in a tracksuit and Nottingham Forest football shirt. His skin is darkened with brown foundation. He wears a fake goatee beard and dreadlock wig, into which a huge plastic pineapple has been threaded. His gait is awkward, his expression gormless. This entrance is greeted with a sudden burst of laughter and applause, the sound of recognition, appreciation or enjoyment of the studio audience reacting to the outrageous incongruity of seeing Lee depicted – or Baddiel transformed – thus. This response can be explained by the series' repeated mockery of Lee's hairstyle, and his recent run of poor form. Through these televisual repetitions, the audience – in-studio and, by extension, at home – was primed to quickly decode the pineapple reference and from it to recognise Lee. To borrow Zheng and Stear's (2023) terminology, this is a fictive deployment of an ongoing, racially coded form of mockery at Lee's expense. It is disingenuous to suggest, as some contemporary commenters did (for instance, Sheehan, 1996; Joseph, 1996), that these are only jokes about a bad or impractical hairstyle, since dreadlocks are a distinctively racialised signifier connected in the UK to the Caribbean diaspora, hence Thompson's identification that the caricature was 'mocking Rastas'.

The sketch incorporates a montage comprising archive footage of Lee's missed goal opportunities which ends with a medium-shot profile of him with hands over his face in disappointment. A slow dissolve reveals Baddiel-as-Lee, making the same gesture, his pineapple head carefully aligned with Lee's fading silhouette. As discussed in Chapter 2, the use of photographic or archive imagery creates a line of continuity between the real persona and the caricature, aided here by the dissolve edit. This visual joke constructs a parallel between the Baddiel caricature and Lee's (racialised) physicality, as well as the aspect of his footballing career the show had repeatedly made fun of, his frustrating inability to finish goals. The sketch includes visual gags in which Baddiel-as-Lee fails to perform a series of apparently easy physical activities, such as missing a rubbish bin at close range, dropping a sugarcube outside of a teacup, or failing to start a Newton's cradle toy. The overt target of the caricature, then, is Lee as a clumsy or below-par sportsman. But this caricature signature is delivered via both blackface and the personification of a racist visual metaphor.

The poetic voice in *The Fruit of the Spirit* poignantly captures the shame of complicity in the racist televisual caricature by joining in with the terrace chant it inspired. First speculating whether Lee prayed that his children would be protected from the humiliation he was suffering, it goes on to ask:

> ... Should I tell mine
> I filled my lungs with '90s minstrelsy
> and sang, a teen lost in lads' mag England?

The 'lads mag', including titles like *Loaded* and *FHM*, reflected a new cultural formation in the 1990s, one characterised by a resurgence of hegemonic masculinity combined with a tolerance for immaturity, encapsulated by *Loaded*'s tagline 'for men who should know better' (Benwell, 2002). Leon Hunt identifies *Fantasy Football League*'s 'homosocial atmosphere' as characteristic of the trend of 'laddishness' in 'post-alternative' comedy (2013, 11), and Sarah Godfrey describes it as a 'televisual equivalent' of men's magazines (2022, 94). The show's 'post-pub' 11.15 p.m. broadcast time, scruffily furnished set dressed to resemble a bachelor pad, casual costuming and improvised humour style combined to recreate the lifestyle Skinner and Baddiel could be assumed to share as real-world flatmates. Its spontaneity and informality exhibited 'lad culture's' supposed authenticity, ordinariness and unpretentiousness, where its subject matter reaches to the very heart of 'new lad' culture; as Rosalind Gill puts it, 'football is not simply one of new lad's interests but has also been profoundly important in his very constitution' (2003, 53). In contrast to the retrospective shame of having engaged in laddish banter evoked in *The Fruit of the Spirit*, Bethan Benwell suggests that the term 'sham*eless*' best captures the tone of new lad discourse. The word bears both the positive meaning of openness and the absence of hypocrisy, and negative, disapproving connotations, though 'with a possible hint of amused (though distanced) admiration' (2002, 151–2).

Much of the scholarship on 'lad culture' has emphasised its sexism, homophobia and racism, described by Garry Whannel as 'lurking close to the surface' in *Fantasy Football League* but, 'excused as postmodern irony' (2000, 297). Irony produces meaning at both literal and non-literal levels, which creates a sense of ambiguity, but it is also a 'useful strategy for disclaiming responsibility for politically unpalatable sentiments' (Benwell, 2002, 163). Irony's power is in accommodating a range of responses, and its pleasure is in 'trying on' different readings and being able to discriminate between them. Benwell describes this as 'double-voicing', where two sets of contradictory ideologies can co-exist, preserving 'masculine values' while 'keeping political sensitivity intact' (2002, 164). I have argued previously that televisual caricature (as manifested in historical comedies such as *Horrible Histories* (CBBC, 2009–24) and *Drunk History UK* (Comedy Central UK, 2015–17)) can work as postmodern representations of historical figures, making the positive case for irony as a means of encouraging critical historiographical readings (Andrews, 2019). In these cases, the televisual caricatures trace a path through 'official' and 'counter-official' histories, generating humour from the gaps between them. Modifying this argument slightly could help to explain the logic of the 'politically incorrect', transgressive humour of the Jason Lee caricature. Where 'officially' racist discourse is not tolerated in an ethos of liberal diversity, a 'counter-official', ironic adoption of the racist practice of blackface is 'permissible' because audiences are anticipated to approach it with 'knowingness' and to recognise the lack of racist intent. The caricature is addressed to an ideal viewer with the knowledge and disposition to manage this polysemy (see Chapter 2), though as Benwell (2002, 164) notes, purveyors of 'lads mags' sometimes found themselves in the invidious position of needing to distance themselves from consumers of their products who 'incorrectly' read only at the literal level. To be clear: this is not an attempt to excuse this blackface caricature. I concur with Brand (2023) that such instances of 'ironic' blackface caricature are 'weakly reflexive'. The claim of postmodern irony here is to invite its audience to relax, to postpone offence, not to take themselves, or others, so seriously. Rather than turning our critical radar up, we are invited to switch it off.

Unlike most skit caricatures, Baddiel's Jason Lee impersonation had an extra-televisual afterlife, one vividly captured in *The Fruit of the Spirit*. The poem evokes the most immediate effect of the sketch, the translation of the 'pineapple on his head' from absurd televisual imagery to football terrace chant, aided by the uptake of the 'pineapple' epithet by sports journalists.[4] For Lee, this was not harmless fun, but had substantial consequences for his career. In May 1996, four months after the first appearance of the caricature, Lee was transfer listed (made a candidate for sale to another club) at Nottingham Forest. His manager, Frank Clark, directly attributed this to *Fantasy Football League*, arguing that Lee had been 'victimised' by the programme and his performance had been affected (Low, 1996). The show's producers rebuffed this claim, criticising Clark's decision to transfer list Lee and to draw media attention to his problems and stating that both he and Lee had declined offers to appear on the show. Commenting on this in July 1996, Lee said it was a matter of principle, as was his decision to keep his distinctive hairstyle (Custis, 1996). He asserted that, while he laughed along at first, the comedians had gone too far, describing the negative impact the mockery had had on his family. Lee's reaction displayed an interesting mix of the various responses to satire in relation to dignity outlined by Giselinde Kuipers (2015). Given the media scrutiny it engendered, it was not possible for him to ignore the caricature. The refusal to appear on *Fantasy Football League* meant that Lee did not take the option of visibly laughing along or joking back but also avoided implicitly endorsing the caricature. He did not publicly show anger, shame or withdrawal; indeed, keeping his dreadlocks can be read

---

[4] A Lexis+ UK search for "Jason Lee" and "Pineapple" (date limited to pre-2020 to eliminate results related to Baddiel's apology – see below) generates 200 results. Only one of these results predates the *Fantasy Football League* sketch.

as an act of defiance. By acknowledging its emotional effect on his family, Lee attempted to neutralise the effects of the caricature through (re-)humanisation. While this left him vulnerable to claims that he could not take a joke, which is a common means of discrediting actors in the (British) public sphere, it also helped him to maintain dignity.

A year later, Lee's wife Ann contributed to a Channel 4 *Cutting Edge* documentary titled *Footballers' Wives*. Compared to the other, wealthier, footballing families depicted, the Lees represent the insecurity caused by a career trajectory over which players have little control. Their narrative arc concerns the uncertainty caused by Lee's place in the transfer list, and the prospect of his sale to another club forcing a relocation from Nottingham, where Ann wishes to make her permanent home. If Clark's assertion that the decision to transfer list Lee was causally related to the televisual caricature is truthful, then *Footballers' Wives* documents its direct material and personal consequences for his family. The documentary specifically addresses the *Fantasy Football League* sketch. A medium long shot in the Lees' living room shows their (rather small) television displaying the beginning of the caricature sketch. In voiceover, Ann queries the public assumption that all football players are highly paid, a sentiment congruent with the visual setting in the Lees' modest family home. The juxtaposition of Ann's candid assertion that they are not as wealthy as is commonly believed with images of the televisual caricature provide an implied refutation of the argument that footballers are rich, powerful and therefore 'fair game' for ridicule. Ann is framed in closeup as she watches the sketch, capturing an expression of displeasure and anxiety, and certainly no humour (Fig. 4.1). The next shot provides a reverse angle, showing the images on the television screen as she watches, an invitation for viewers to empathise with Ann and view the caricature, literally, from her point of view (Fig. 4.2).

Ann notes that Lee became 'more famous for his haircut than for his football', attributing this to what she refers to as 'the Skinner and Baddiel show', a discursive framing that holds the

Fig. 4.1 Ann Lee watches images of her husband portrayed as a caricature, *Cutting Edge: Footballers' Wives*

Fig. 4.2 The Jason Lee caricature, as shown from Ann's point of view, *Cutting Edge: Footballers' Wives*

comedians directly accountable. While she insists that the sketch had not 'wrecked his career', she acknowledges that the 'pineapple' chants affected him and contributed to him not being chosen for Nottingham Forest's first team. Her reflections on these events are delivered matter-of-factly, but their inclusion in a broader discussion about her (currently unfulfilled) aspirations for Jason's career lends them a sense of pathos. By mediating these events from Ann's perspective, *Footballers' Wives* affectively documents how this televisual caricature, an artefact of the cultural public sphere, had spilled over into the Lees' private lives. This section of the documentary closes on an image of Jason, now with a shaved head, lying on his couch and (it is implied) watching the caricature sketch. Given its placement in the documentary's narrative structure at a moment in which his family's precarity has been exposed, the image of a prone Lee suggests not relaxed contemplation of a trivial, amusing television skit, but vulnerability and disempowerment.

Baddiel and Skinner were among the public figures who issued apologies for past racist acts after June 2020, and the Jason Lee caricature continues to be a topic on which they are drawn by journalists. In a 2022 interview, Skinner reflected on the sketch with disbelief: 'I still don't know why one or both of us … or *someone* there didn't say "what the fuck is happening?"' (Jonze, 2022). This echoes Marvin Thompson's reading of the line 'a comedian blacked up' with an incredulous questioning tone in the video for *The Fruit of the Spirit*. In a short essay written for the Poetry Society, Thompson rhetorically implicates television as an industry in the hurt caused by the blackface caricatures, asking 'where were the apologies from the TV executives who greenlighted the shows?' (Wafa, 2020). While acknowledging personal culpability for writing and performing in the sketch, Skinner pointed out that 'the BBC watched the show before it went out and OKed it. They were supposed to be a guiding hand' (Jonze, 2022). Lee similarly challenged Baddiel during a wide-ranging 2022 podcast interview: 'as much as I hold you accountable, I hold so many more accountable … Was there anybody at any stage that said, hold on a minute, you're going too far?' (AbsoluteLee Podcast, 2022). These questions shift the emphasis from Baddiel and Skinner's responsibility as individuals to a broader institutional culture within television production, one which would tolerate, ignore or even fail to notice these instances of racism. Baddiel answers Lee's question by pointing out that there was 'an acceptability to that kind of comedy' in the culture of the time, though stressing this as explanation rather than excuse. Jack Black describes such discursive moves as acts of 'contextual deferment' in which 'associating one's actions with a particular (historical) period can help to contextually distance one's former Self from the present and thus relativise it' (2020, 85). Skinner and Baddiel's apologies are couched in terms that accept personal responsibility while also providing this sense of formal deferment from their past selves and implicating the broader culture, including the institutional culture of the BBC, in the blackface caricature.

Though his appearance on Lee's podcast marked the first time the men met face to face, Baddiel had made public apologies for the caricature several times prior to this, in print, via his Twitter account and in his bestselling, book-length essay *Jews Don't Count* (2021). On the same day as the podcast interview was released, Channel 4 broadcast a TV adaptation, *David Baddiel: Jews Don't Count* (2022). The thesis of *Jews Don't Count* is that the progressive left tends to overlook or downgrade antisemitism by comparison with other forms of discrimination. In both documentary and book, Baddiel explores, and counters, some explanations for this phenomenon: that Jewish people occupy a contradictory imagined high/low social, cultural and political status, the assumption that they have greater power or wealth than other minorities, that 'passing' as white confers the privileges associated with whiteness or that antisemitism should be classified as religious intolerance rather than a form of racism. In the documentary, Baddiel rehearses some of these arguments in interviews with Jewish celebrities, expanding the book's themes by adding other experiences and voices. This is interspersed with sequences in which he stands at the centre of a white room, photographed in black and white, directly addressing the camera as he outlines his case, effectively remediating the 'voice' of the book via a style that is visibly distinct from the other parts of the documentary. In one of these, which appears as the transition to a commercial break, Baddiel looks to camera and says, 'meanwhile some of you – certainly those of you who populate my online life – will be saying "yeah yeah Baddiel, banging on about bloody Jews again but … this you?"' This is accompanied by a still from the *Fantasy Football League* sketch occupying one half of the screen, the other taken up by text that reads '#ThisYou?' That the Jason Lee caricature can operate structurally in the programme as a teaser to encourage audiences to return from an advertising break demonstrates the level of notoriety it has enjoyed in its online afterlife, the media interest in it and, as Baddiel goes on to explore, the rhetorical significance it has accrued in social media debates he has engaged in about antisemitism.

The #ThisYou? sequence is followed by a reiteration of Baddiel's apology for the Lee caricature, visualised in the black-and-white, direct-address style. He states, 'I understand this now to be part of a very bad, racist tradition.' In including the word 'now' the statement allows both an admission of culpability and a mitigation based on 'epistemological ignorance', since the history and meaning of blackface was not understood 'then'. Baddiel then remarks on his history of apologising for the caricature and reiterates by slowly and carefully enunciating 'I am sorry.' The apology is restated visually, in large, black, plain-font, all-caps text superimposed over the white background. This presentational style projects an intended sense of seriousness and sincerity for this message, though it also has a functional use in the documentary's argument. Baddiel goes on to argue that his apologies have had little effect on the frequency with which the image appears on his Twitter timeline, in response to his statements about the discrimination, exclusion or social disadvantages experienced by Jewish people. This is illustrated by the screen filling with examples of Tweets in which the caricature is evoked to undermine Baddiel's campaign against antisemitism. The implication, in

Baddiel's reading of these tweets, is that the Jason Lee caricature is being presented as an invalidation of his ability to speak about racism. The televisual caricature has endured far beyond its original context, both medial and sociocultural. It has transformed into a meme and, as Baddiel describes it in the book, a 'trump card' (2021, 70) in online debates about the relationship between antisemitism and racism, one in which he has become a vocal interlocutor and therefore a target for critique.

In both *Jews Don't Count* and his interview with Jason Lee, Baddiel pinpoints a moment of clarity for him when, in 2004, he became the target of a televisual caricature. In the comedy sketch show *Bo Selecta*, Baddiel was performed by Leigh Francis in a parody of his popular light entertainment show *Baddiel and Skinner Unplanned* (ITV, 2000–5). Baddiel is depicted as an outrageous caricature of a Jewish man, with a large nose, dark beard, curly sidelocks and a white kippah, who speaks in a cod Middle Eastern accent and encourages a caricature of Frank Skinner to 'call me Jew, they [the studio audience] like it when you call me Jew'. Outlining the personal effect this had on him to Lee, Baddiel admits both that he hated it, and that it 'shifted [something] in me: "this is how Jason Lee must have felt"' (AbsoluteLee Podcast, 2022). In *David Baddiel: Jews Don't Count*, this private resonance of the *Bo Selecta* caricature is missing from Baddiel's analysis, and instead he focuses on its position in the cultural public sphere. He argues that, since Francis is not Jewish, to portray him in this fashion is racist, looking directly to camera to issue a direct challenge to the viewer. In the book, this is included in a broader discussion of the widespread practice of Jewish characters being played by actors who are not Jewish in film and television. Baddiel compares the use of comically exaggerated signifiers of Jewishness in some performances with the practice of blackface by asking, 'when you cartoon the Jewishness, and you yourself are not Jewish, what is that if not minstrelsy in another form?' (2021, 65). A flaw in this argument is to evacuate minstrelsy of its historical specificity and its role in maintaining the 'controlling images' that provide ideological justification for the oppression of African

Americans and, in its cultural export, Black people elsewhere. The broader point stands; that is to challenge the appropriateness of cross-cultural impersonation on the grounds of inauthenticity in dramatic portrayals, and of ridicule and/or the perpetuation of harmful stereotypes in comic ones. As *Jews Don't Count*'s inclusion of many examples of caricatures and cartoons attests to, such images and performances have contributed significantly to cultural assumptions that have led to the marginalisation and exclusion of Jewish people.

The legacy of the Jason Lee caricature demonstrates the delicate interplay between the (cultural) public sphere and private realm. For Jason Lee, who has understandably sought to dispute the destructive effect it had on his personal life and career, the caricature has become, against his will, a core part of his public persona. In later years this had the positive outcome of making him an authoritative voice on matters of equality, diversity and inclusion in sport. For Marvin Thompson, the caricature provides a powerful metaphor for the toxicity of 1990s lad culture and its perpetuation of casual racism through the tool of playful irony. For David Baddiel, it has mutated into a meme used in bad-faith rebuttals to his campaign against antisemitism, which has impeded his arguments and compromised the reception of his message. Anamik Saha (2020) argues, following Gavan Titley (2019), that in the contemporary media environment which depends commercially on attention and the production of a vast stream of content, the politics of representation has itself become media content, which serves an economic as well as an ideological function. The Jason Lee caricature, and the volume of debate it has generated across social media, podcasting, books, documentaries and other media spaces, provides a strong example of this. In June 2020, the politics-of-representation-as-media-content found a prominent iteration in the trend of the celebrity and institutional apology for racism. The effect on media went beyond this, to the very availability of and access to past instances of racist televisual caricature via television archives. It is to these cancellations we now turn.

Afterlives of televisual caricature: Apologies and archival absences

On 5 June 2020, amidst a global outpouring of grief and anger over the murder of George Floyd eleven days earlier, comedian Leigh Francis made a candid video for his Instagram channel reflecting on a 'weird few days' he had experienced. He had been the subject of a social media backlash against the programme that had launched his television career. *Bo Selecta* was a comedy sketch show that satirised popular culture of the early 2000s. The series ridiculed the excesses of millennial celebrity culture, partly through its central character Avid Merrion (played by Francis), a libidinous fan whose unhealthy obsession with personalities from TV and pop music is the central comic conceit of the series. Celebrities frequently appeared as guests on the show, a valuable opportunity to demonstrate their sense of humour and ability to laugh at themselves, which had become a *sine qua non* of an early 2000s British popular culture strongly influenced by postmodern irony and a backlash against 'political correctness'. The tone of the show, in keeping with much comedy of the time, was irreverent, deliberately poking at the boundaries of taste with scatological, sexualised and defiantly politically incorrect humour.

Nowhere is this more apparent than in the key comic innovation of the show, the performance of deliberately crude celebrity caricatures through ill-fitting rubber masks and silly, inaccurate impressions. Many of these entailed Francis, a white Brit, impersonating people of colour from the US and UK, including television presenters Trisha Goddard and Oprah Winfrey, and popstars Michael Jackson, Melanie Brown (Mel B of the Spice Girls) and, most notoriously, Craig David. While they do not adopt the specific performance or visual traditions of minstrelsy – there is no sense, for example, of the 'virtuosic imitation' – these impersonations do create a concealing/revealing mask and engage in racial spectacularisation in equivalent ways. As the social media commenters to whom Francis's Instagram video responded pointed out, *Bo Selecta*'s caricatures present blackface in a modified guise.

Importantly, as Jack Black puts it, *Bo Selecta*'s caricatures of Black people were 'characterized by the stereotypical representation of these individuals through popular racialized tropes' (2020, 83). Troublingly, though they bore only tenuous relation to their 'real' celebrity target, this 'tenuity was clearly recognisable in the characters that mimicked and accentuated popular racial impersonations' (Black, 2020, 83). This is particularly noticeable in the caricature of Goddard, who Francis performed with an exaggerated, often incomprehensible Jamaican accent peppered with phrases associated with the Caribbean diaspora such as 'rice and peas' or 'lickle'. The portrayal is clearly distinct from the real Goddard, whose public persona was, thanks to her daily talk show, one of a tough but empathetic mediator who speaks with a gentle London accent. Francis's Winfrey speaks in a low, growling Southern US accent and repeatedly expresses preference for fried chicken and other soul food. Jackson's famously soft-spoken voice is replaced by a vocal style borrowed from popular representations of urban Blackness, such as Blaxploitation cinema or gangsta rap. The Mel B caricature depicts her as masculinised and vulgar, drawing on cultural associations between Northern English working-class women and failures of 'correct' femininity and sexuality. These tropes, though specific to the British milieu, are analogous to some of the excessively sexualised or classed 'controlling images' that have perpetuated the oppression of Black women.

Pop star Craig David is by far the most featured caricature in *Bo Selecta*, which drew its title from a lyric in his breakout hit single 'Re-Rewind (The Crowd Say Bo Selecta)' (1999). The caricature portrays him as infantile, incontinent and uncool. While the vocal impression is deliberately inaccurate, replacing David's Southampton accent with Yorkshire dialect, the costuming and mask design mimics David's signature look, including carefully styled facial hair, designer-casual clothes, tightly braided corn rows and a beanie hat. The introductory intertitle for 'Craig David on Tour' segments of the show in its second series spoofs the album cover for his debut *Born to Do It* (Fig. 4.3), while the

Cancelling Televisual Caricature 135

Fig. 4.3 Bo Selecta caricatures the star image of Craig David

soundtrack is a close pastiche of his hit song 'Seven Days'. The caricature lampoons David by having him frequently refer to himself in the third person in a singing tone, a characteristic of the UK garage genre, which combined jungle, R&B and house, and typically consisted of singing and rapping over electronically produced beats. The caricature ridiculed an element of UK popular culture of the early 2000s which was substantially associated with Black British identity. The intent – and certainly Francis's public defence – of these caricatures is to create a comedic disjunction between the celebrity figure and their *Bo Selecta* depiction (Delaney, 2006). However, in reproducing and not interrogating the stereotypes on which their humour depends, they meet Luvell Anderson's (2023) criteria at least for 'racially insensitive' humour and Amanda N. Brand's (2023) definition of 'racist blackface caricature'.

Francis's Instagram apology offers a stark admission that, when he portrayed Black people in the show, he 'didn't think anything about it' and 'didn't realise how offensive it was', an appeal to both 'white innocence' and 'white epistemological ignorance'. He apologises for 'any upset I caused' and concludes, 'I guess we're all on a learning journey'. Jack Black describes the form of this apology as one of 'reflexive disavowal', which 'can be seen to reflect the recognition that his former performances were largely offensive, [but] this recognition remains tied to a disavowal of the very position from which these performances were made' (2020, 84–5). There are other discursive distancing devices employed throughout the video. Francis opens by introducing himself as a person who is better known as a 'character' (chat show host Keith Lemon) whom he plays on television. Television is here presented as a fictionalising, distorting medium by comparison with the social media video, positioned as a more authentic mediator of Francis's true self. This suggests that the actions for which Francis is being held accountable were really performed by a different person, a fictional character invented by and for television, implicating the medium itself in the transgressions. As Chiara Bucaria and Luca Barra (2016, 11) argue, taboo comedy works within television's perpetual balance between 'showing the truth' and the manipulation of reality, and here the medium's inherent inauthenticity is used as a justification for an offensive representation. Francis also couches the apology in historical terms, reflecting that 'back then' he did not understand the ramifications of his actions. This rhetorically constructs a deferment or 'postponement of one's intentions or actions *onto* the context in which they occurred to position oneself as a "victim of circumstances"' (Black, 2020, 90). This is not to suggest that Francis's apologies were insincere or cynically timed (as, for example, David has), but to point out that the manner of their framing was to implicate television medially and institutionally alongside the personal responsibility for the racist caricatures.

As is familiar from the example of Jason Lee above, targets of *Bo Selecta* (for example, Trisha Goddard) pointed not only to Francis's personal culpability for these blackface caricatures, but to the systemic racism at the industrial level that enabled them to be broadcast (BBC News, 2020). It is important, therefore, to consider the industrial context in which *Bo Selecta* was made. Lloyd Peters and Sue Becker (2010) describe the 2000s as the period of 'New British Comedy', one in which a seemingly more permissive commissioning climate enabled the broadcast of 'edgy' comedy.

Channel 4 had specialised in boundary-pushing, experimental comedy since the late 1990s, much of which was produced, like *Bo Selecta*, by Talkback Thames, a comedy specialist production company that made *Brass Eye* (1997–2001), *The 11 O'clock Show* (1998–2000) and its progeny *Da Ali G Show* (2000–4). *Bo Selecta* was broadcast on a Friday evening at 11 p.m., which had become a typical schedule position on Channel 4 for such comedy. The channel was, during this period, pursuing younger audiences (18- to 34-year-olds) as a means of fulfilling their public service requirement to address underserved audiences and provide an alternative to other commercial and public service provision (Brown, 2007). According to Channel 4's 2003 Annual report, more than half of *Bo Selecta*'s audience were aged 18–34 (Channel 4, 2003, 37). The fact that this demographic is hard to reach and particularly appealing to advertisers was commercially expedient for Channel 4, at its audience peak during the early 2000s thanks in large part to its hit reality show *Big Brother* (2000–10) (Brown, 2007, 304–14). *Big Brother* is a key satirical target of *Bo Selecta*. Its celebrity-obsessed protagonist first appeared a character on spin-off E4 show *Big Brother's Little Brother* (2001–10), and his fascination with the reality programme, and its host Davina McCall (who also appears as a caricature) is a recurring joke throughout the series. *Bo Selecta* and *Big Brother* provided Channel 4 with a useful synergy, with the former generating attention to and greater prominence for the latter even as it made fun of its excesses.

Bo Selecta benefitted Channel 4 in several ways. It attracted a valuable audience and directed significant attention to the channel. As with *Spitting Image* (a programme it was occasionally compared with), tie-in merchandise, including a novelty Christmas record called 'Proper Crimbo' (2003), helped to sustain the position of the show in popular culture (see Chapter 3). Its cultural influence far outweighed the actual size of the audience, which peaked at 2.82m in June 2004 (BARB, undated b). Although it received a decidedly mixed critical reception, the show was a unique and innovative televisual prospect for its time, in alignment with the channel's core values. Indicators of this congruence with the Channel 4 brand can be found in its 2003 Annual Report. One page features a cartoon illustration of Chief Executive Mark Thompson, standing in the centre of a busy office, holding a Channel 4 branded clipboard, just beneath which is a bust of the *Bo Selecta* caricature of Craig David (Channel 4, 2003, 4). Another is dedicated to a nonsensical 'essay' written in Avid Merrion's voice (Channel 4, 2003, 17).

The moment of *Bo Selecta* coincided with changes to Channel 4's approach to the representation – on and off screen – of people of racialised minorities. Sarita Malik (2008) characterises this as moving from a policy of 'multiculturalism' to 'mainstreaming'. The year 2002 marked a totemic point in this shift, with the closure of the Multicultural Programming Department, through which much of its commissioning of programming from Black-led production companies was previously organised. The rationale was that the department was no longer needed, as minority representation's future lay in mainstream programming. Malik (2008, 348) suggests this marked a loss of antiracism at an institutional level typical of the mid 2000s, indicative of a broader social move in the UK towards post-multiculturalism. At Channel 4, this was part of a longer process in which, after its funding formula shifted in 1993 from a fixed stipend to a more conventional commercial-model based on advertising sales, minority programming became increasingly marginalised. Working in a competitive television marketplace, Channel 4 began in the 1990s to operate on a 'preferred supplier' model of commissioning from larger, trusted independent production companies, which tended not to include Black independents. Talkback Thames *was* a preferred supplier, though it had been 'under a cloud' in the early 2000s thanks to a controversial episode of *Brass Eye* (Brown, 2007, 229–30). Malik argues that during its first decade, Channel 4 presented diversity as 'something edgy, modern, fluid and decentred' (2008, 344), a description that maps onto the channel's later alignment of provocative comedies that poke at cultural sensitivities with its brand values of experimentation and risk taking. In 2008, I mounted a defence of Channel 4 from the perspective of a person from the

18–34 demographic it aimed to serve, citing its continuing commitment to young audiences, and to innovation in programme style and form. On the mainstreaming of minority representation, I suggested that it was a legitimate policy, on the grounds that programming intended to address minority audiences could isolate and alienate those it aimed to serve (Andrews, 2008). I was wrong about this, because I had not properly considered the content or tone of mainstream programming and its (implicit and explicit) exclusions or misrepresentations of people from racialised minorities, as well as other marginalised groups.

New British Comedy reacted against 'political correctness', positioned as a 'principled stand' against censorship (Peters and Becker, 2010, 193). Comedy's relationship with free speech has become a point of contention in the context of the culture wars (Andrews and Frame, 2025). There has been an oppositional reaction to so-called 'cancel culture' from comedians who, positioning themselves as provocateurs, deliver jokes on socially sensitive topics with the intention of causing offence (Goldstraw, 2023). Brett Mills (2016) borrows the phrase 'special freedom' from a historical code of standards used by the UK regulator to explain the representational specificity of comedy. He argues that while regulators acknowledge the powerful social role of comedy, it can 'say and do that which would be unacceptable in other, more serious modes' (2016, 224). Comedy's role as part of the cultural public sphere endows it with a licence to push boundaries further than 'serious' discourse can (see Chapter 2). However, as explored in Chapter 3, compliance, especially the governance of the politics of representation, has tightened over the 2010s to recognise the needs of a culturally diverse society, or, from the opposing perspective, to repress culturally unsanctioned ('politically incorrect') opinion. Shifts in institutional attitudes to comic offence make it possible to argue that *Fantasy Football League* or *Bo Selecta* are 'of their time' as a means of explaining/excusing their employment of blackface caricature, evidencing Barra and Bucaria's claim that 'taboos tend to be relative and not absolute' (2016, 7). The 'special freedom' of comedy varies according to broader cultural consensus about the acceptable limits of ridicule, one which has become strained in the polarised political culture of the 2020s.

The historical relativity of the limits of comic acceptability is made particularly obvious in the retroactive censorship of television comedy with racist themes or representations (Black, 2021, 109). For *Bo Selecta*, this occurred in June 2020, as the series was removed from Channel 4's online video-on-demand service All 4, part of a wave of content take downs prompted by Black Lives Matter protests that included episodes of *Little Britain* (BBC Three/One, 2003–6), *Scrubs* (NBC/ABC 2001–10) and *30 Rock* (NBC, 2006–13). Channel 4 issued a brief statement explaining the withdrawal from their site: 'We support Leigh in his decision to reflect on *Bo' Selecta* in light of recent events and we've agreed with him to remove the show from the All 4 archive' (Herr, 2020, 23). Channel 4's statement aligns its corporate actions with Francis's apology and disavowal, a similarly distancing move that separates the current channel from its history of broadcasting these blackface caricatures. As Amanda N. Brand argues of similar removals in the US, this is implicitly presented as 'an act of racial reckoning or correcting a past mistake' (2023, 225). This rings somewhat hollow when we remember that as recently as December 2019, Channel 4 commissioned a ninety-minute special *What a F***in Year on TV with Mel B and Mel B* (E4, 2019) that featured Francis as his Mel B caricature, alongside the real Melanie Brown.[5] The All 4 removal might therefore be read as Channel 4 engaging in what Brand calls 'shallow investments in racial justice' (2023, 216), in distinct contrast to the corporate image of the broadcaster which emphasises its authentic commitment to equality, diversity and inclusion (Channel 4, undated). Brand critiques the archival removals that occurred in the wake of the murder of George Floyd on two grounds. First, she suggests that the blanket

---

[5] Brown was a frequent contributor to *Bo Selecta*, an example of Kuiper's (2015) 'laughing along' response that helps maintain dignity but risks endorsing the satirical representation.

discarding of all racially risky materials meant withdrawing critical and satirical representations, thus 'reinforc[ing] colorblind racism and obscur[ing] antiracist discourses' (2023, 216). While I am less convinced than Brand by satire as a justification for blackface performance, I agree that a more nuanced discussion was required than was achieved through these removals. Second, she argues that

> Blackface removal appears to shift choice and control back into the hands of media distribution companies ... as these platforms serve their own political and financial interests by leaving untouched programmes that serve their bottom line and censoring those that threaten it. (2023, 216)

In this reading, removing such portrayals from publicly accessible archives is not an empowering or protective gesture in the name of inclusion, but a cynical, cowardly act of repression and negation of corporate responsibility for the existence of these images. As Racquel Gates pointed out, keeping 'problematic' content offline prevents proper engagement with how it was made in the first place, an attempt to erase rather than confront the past (qtd in Framke, 2020).

Orna Herr articulates the question regarding blackface removals from public media archives thus: 'Is "disappearing" shows that contain language and content that is now more widely deemed as offensive an appropriate and effective response or is it censorship and an attempt to rewrite history?' (2020, 22). The presence or absence of materials in public archives is, in this view, a matter of the politics of heritage. Kristyn Gorton and Joanne Garde-Hansen argue that there has been a recent move towards British television heritage, one that is:

> becoming increasingly built on the technologized ability to self-reflexively produce a history of television inside and outside of the industry (e.g. the repurposing of television archives online by broadcasters as well as fans, YouTube playlists, the re-emergence of old idents, or the monumentalization of both popular culture). (2019, 13)

Broadcasters' public opening of their content libraries, as well as their sales of old programming to third-party content aggregators, has become incorporated into British television heritage, a means of remembering television's past. Discussing the commercial role of archives in the contemporary media industry, Gorton and Garde-Hansen distinguish between 'now nostalgia', which is 'acceptable, profitable, scalable and responsive to new (global) audiences in new ways' (2019, 16), and 'not now nostalgia', 'not in and of this present time strategy, stored away in the past, too much of the past' (17). Channel 4's decision to remove blackface caricature from the archive is a gesture that designates it as belonging to 'not now nostalgia', to separate it from the contemporary corporate image and consign it to a past that is no longer expedient to the broadcaster. In the context of the culture wars, appeals to a recent past in which it was (purportedly) culturally permissible to offend are contrasted with 'woke' culture in which 'politically incorrect' views are said to be censored. The cancellation of the content itself becomes the subject of scrutiny rather than the moral implications of its existence in the first place.

Moreover, as Gorton and Garde-Hansen note, television history is also produced and maintained outside of the television industry. My ability to write at such length about *Fantasy Football League*, for example, has been aided by the availability of the episode on YouTube, where it was uploaded unofficially. The presence of the show in 'rogue archives' has enabled the digital afterlife of the Jason Lee caricature (de Kosnik, 2016). It is not possible to know the motivations behind such activities, and therefore to gauge the extent to which it is a purposeful resistance against the 'politically correct' cancellation of such images from 'official' archives. However, the continuing availability of the material online renders the removal of blackface caricature from institutional archives ineffective as a means of protecting the public from its harmful effects. Leaving the curation of these images to 'rogue archivists' risks redoubling their harms, as they can be recontextualised as taboo content to be circulated and appreciated *for* their racism, not despite it. To remove access to previous instances of blackface caricature can be read as a strategic attempt to encourage cultural amnesia, or what Paul Connerton calls 'prescriptive forgetting', an 'expression of the wish that past actions should not just be forgiven but forgotten' (2008, 62). To prevent access to certain content, then, is to express a desire to foreclose such memories. Blackface caricatures are blights on television history, and to render them publicly inaccessible is to inhibit critical re-evaluation. Removing this content from public circulation is a tokenistic gesture, a means of skirting rightful critique of these representations and the industries that produced them.

An alternative method to the wholesale removal of racist content was taken by HBOMax in relation to *Gone With the Wind* (1939) and its patronising, stereotypical depictions of African Americans in the antebellum South. It was temporarily withdrawn from the service in the immediate aftermath of George Floyd's death. By 25 June 2020 it was returned to the platform with a disclaimer acknowledging the racism in its depictions of African American characters, alongside explanatory video material that discussed the history of complaint about the racism in the film, from its release onwards, a means of forestalling the unsatisfactory argument that these were simply images 'of their time'. Rather than simply whisking these artefacts away from public view and hoping that their invisibility will entail their forgetting, this approach acknowledges multiple layers of injustice: not only in the creation of these images to begin with, but also in the suppression of complaint against them. The BBC has similarly attempted a level of redress for *The Black and White Minstrel Show*, both as part of its centenary history website authored by historian David Hendy (2022), and in a feature documentary, *David Harewood on Blackface* (2023), both of which confront the corporation's complacency and condescension towards Black audiences. Blackface televisual caricatures, as this chapter has explored, have their own complex afterlives, which are better served by encouraging scrutiny of their place in television history than by obscuring them from view.

Conclusion

This chapter has, via a consideration of blackface impersonation, explored the negative obverse of televisual caricature as it was presented in Chapter 2. Televisual caricature was analysed in that chapter for its positive contribution to the cultural public sphere as a means by which powerful or influential figures can be held to account. Achieving this through deformation and ridicule is inevitably cruel. The benefit of greater cultural prominence for caricature targets comes at considerable personal cost to well-being and identity, to a sense of self. Chapter 2 also argues for the sophistication of televisual caricature, in contrast to outward appearance, because of its address to an engaged audience that it demands must draw on cultural knowledge to decode and appreciate its meaning, the 'beholder's share'. This chapter has considered the outcome when such 'knowledges' are drawn from discriminatory, oppressive and misrepresenting stereotypes about social groups. The address of caricature depends not only on knowledge but on disposition, the 'prescription' of certain attitudes in the viewer. While such dispositions can be subversive or oppositional, a way of rejecting or critiquing dominant power structures, they can also be oppressive and prejudiced. Televisual caricature often employs mechanisms of ironic distancing, gesturing to the viewer to suspend their disbelief while simultaneously accepting the truth claims connected to the impersonation of a real figure. Irony has been used to excuse offensive caricature, to present the 'moral alibi' of satire (Mondal, 2018) that allows depictions that would be unsanctioned elsewhere in the public sphere.

I see a qualitative distinction between political or social caricature of individuals that depends on a set of knowledges around the public persona of that individual, and a caricature that relies on knowledge of discriminatory and dehumanising tropes associated with specific cultural groups. While I maintain that it is important to trust in the viewer's interpretive capabilities, this is insufficient moral grounds to justify the perpetuation of harmful imagery. To insist on the adoption of the distanced or ironic viewing positionality of the perceiver for the 'correct' interpretation of the caricature is to uphold a social order that renders white experience as the 'neutral' norm from which viewing should take place. This is obviously not to imply that postmodern irony is the exclusive preserve of white people, but to acknowledge the privilege of being able to view racist caricature at a remove, under no risk from its effects. As Anshuman Mondal argues, 'powerful and dominant groups and individuals can easily shrug off offensive speech because despite the performance of offensiveness, such speech does not disturb the structural advantage they enjoy' (2018, 29). The mere 'intention' either to avoid offence or to subvert stereotype cannot exempt racist caricature from culpability, because 'intention' cannot guarantee the effect of racist communication.

The 'cancellation' of blackface televisual caricatures occurred in 2020 as a gesture of solidarity with campaigns against anti-Black racism. It was a flawed response that did not serve the intended purpose of redress for social injustice. David Baddiel's apology to Jason Lee has not ended the online afterlife of the blackface televisual caricature, which continues its use as a meme in arguments about racism and antisemitism. Indeed, Baddiel has subsequently described his frustration with the media's emphasis on his apology to Lee in *Jews Don't Count* on the grounds that it distracted from the key message of the show and shifted the terms of the debate onto anti-Black racism as opposed to antisemitism. Expressing his and (apparently) Lee's mutual desire to put the dispute behind them, Baddiel asks, 'If it's not serving Jason Lee, why am I continually being asked about it?' (qtd in Leith, 2023). Leigh Francis has similarly issued a request that Craig David 'move on' from *Bo Selecta* (Graye, 2023). These are pleas for forgetting that are abetted by the removals of the blackface caricatures from the public archives of broadcasters. This is an attempt to consign the blackface caricatures to a television past, to a 'not now nostalgia' that has no meaningful place in the contemporary cultural public sphere. Though for television institutions these images can no longer work as useful content, they have continued to have a cultural and economic function thanks to the value of the politics of representation in digital media (Titley, 2019; Saha, 2020). The afterlives of these blackface televisual caricatures, their repeated circulation across digital media, their readiness to hand for journalists and social media users, render them ghostly reminders of a shameful recent past, and of the place of television comedy in unthinkingly upholding an unjust status quo. While there exist digitally enabled, counter-official mechanisms for the critique of television heritage, and 'rogue archivists' willing to maintain them, televisual caricature cannot truly be cancelled.

5
Conclusion

TV and Caricature has examined the adaptation for the medium of television of an old representational tradition: the comic portrait that ridicules, however lightly, its subject through distortions of their image. It has explored how TV as a medium, an industry and a part of the cultural public sphere has framed, made and 'cancelled' televisual caricature. Throughout, I have returned to the tensions inherent in caricature teased out in the Introduction. These are caricature's contradictory positioning as a simplified visual form that can compel a critical, sophisticated viewing approach; the form's dual tendency towards character assassination through ridicule and towards ego massage, reaffirming the salience of a public persona; the ability of caricature to be both subversive in its attempt to disempower elites, and conservative in its use of deformation as a form of critique and reinforcement of stereotype; its liminal positioning between claims to facticity, even 'truth', and the obvious fictionality of its exaggerations; and its paradoxical ability to render individuals recognisable through distortion. To conclude, I trace how these themes relate to televisual caricature's meanings, pleasures, function and value, and consider how they may translate into future forms of mediated caricature.

Televisual caricature's meanings are constructed through its address, conveying its subjects' putative 'essences' rapidly. Speed is at the heart of what Eric Herhuth calls 'caricatural logic' (2018), requiring television form to communicate immediately the identity of and attitude towards the caricature subject. This has the effect, as Herhuth notes, of 'bypass[ing] contemplation and induc[ing] fast-paced habitual comprehension' (2018, 629); put another way, of engaging a viewer's 'glance' rather than the reflective 'gaze'. The process relies substantially on the 'beholder's share' (Gombrich, 2002), the knowledges, dispositions and biases a viewer brings with them. While caricatures can demand a scrutinising, sceptical or 'oppositional' viewing position from audiences, they can equally serve hegemonic purposes, perpetuating oppressions, by circulating a visual lexicon of stereotype (Herhuth, 2018; Wanzo, 2020).

The pace and topicality of televisual caricature may appear to give it an evanescent quality, a meaning that lasts only as long as a news cycle. Some, nevertheless, last longer. *Spitting Image*, for example, has proved to play a significant role in how Margaret Thatcher is framed in popular memory, cementing her image as a tough, ruthless leader in ways that may have helped as much as harmed her (Farr, 2018). We can trace its influence in subsequent televisual caricatures of Thatcher, which adopt elements of the caricature signature it helped to establish for her, discussed in Chapter 2. Some blackface televisual caricatures, as outlined in Chapter 4, have had a complex online afterlife, circulated as visual evidence of a recent televisual past to be re-evaluated in the context of an ongoing 'culture war'. Though television institutions have distanced themselves from these images via removals from public content libraries, the unruly archive of the internet has made it impossible for them to disappear completely. Televisual caricatures can, despite the ephemerality of the form, endure.

In response to critiques of the illicit pleasure it offers in ridiculing prominent individuals, British televisual caricature has benefited from a ready-made defence in the shape of its continuation of a long-standing cultural tradition of satire and cartooning. This argument was used by the makers and regulators of *Spitting Image* to justify the crueller elements of its caricature, as described in Chapter 3. Much as *Spitting Image* drew on its place in the historical legacy of satirical form, it would become itself a cultural touchstone used by others to legitimate later televisual caricature.

Leigh Francis, for example cites it as the 'equivalent' of *Bo Selecta* in the 1980s (Delaney, 2006). This lends a level of validity to *Bo Selecta* despite its eschewal of overtly political content. Francis's main target, Craig David, also made the comparison (David, 2022, 69), suggesting that appearing as a *Bo Selecta* caricature marked a similar level of cultural relevance as being transformed into a *Spitting Image* puppet. However, the apoliticism of *Bo Selecta* created, for some, a moral distinction from *Spitting Image*. Journalist Polly Vernon, interviewing David, argued that '*Spitting Image* attacked public servants in a grand, established tradition; those public servants were considerably older than you and, frankly, deserved it. You were very young, and at least somewhat vulnerable by definition, and you didn't deserve it' (2019, 45). The assumption that caricature targets those with power, who are able to withstand its assault on their reputation and dignity is central to the moral defence of the form. Televisual caricature's potential to cruelty and, as explored in Chapter 4, to materially impact the lives of its targets, raises questions about the extent to which its pleasures can be justified. Moral assessments of humour forms in general apply to televisual caricatures, but their liminal status between fact and fiction, even claims of conveying inner 'truths', mean that they carry an extra ethical burden.

Politically, caricature has been celebrated for its function of providing a (qualified) check on the power of elites. Like other satirical content, televisual caricatures can form part of the 'comic public sphere' (Caron, 2021), a fictionalised counterpart to the public sphere. Here, humour and irony are employed to encourage citizens to reflect critically on contemporary politics. The comic public sphere provides a space in which we are reminded of democratic norms that have been eroded in recent years, such as a commitment to truth, facticity and transparency. Televisual caricatures of political figures reaffirm a normative baseline (usually at the liberal centre of politics) by presenting their exaggerated personas as absurd deviations. Consider 'Thatcher's' queasy response to an orthodox expression of human worth in *Psychobitches*, or Alec Baldwin's 'Trump', which highlighted the president's unsuitability for office through imitation of his actual utterances and behaviour (in Chapter 2).

Televisual caricature can perform the contradictory role of reaffirming – via ridicule and exaggeration – the carefully maintained public persona on which contemporary political power is so dependent. Political actors are now trained in the development of a knowable, replicable public 'brand', visible and prominent enough to cut through the increasing 'noise' of a hypermediated world (Bal et al., 2009). Televisual caricatures demonstrate the success of this process by showing the imitability of the persona; from another perspective, they offer 'training manuals' in the creation and performance of political personality. Such caricaturability is an increasingly rare and valuable commodity in an attention economy and a 'post-post-broadcast democracy' (Stier et al., 2022) in which internet intermediaries (social media and search engines in particular) play a more decisive role than 'legacy' forms in the provision of news and information. Indeed, as Herhuth argues, 'today's media environment, with its algorithmic architecture, accelerated flows, and compressed forms of information, seems conducive to more animated, interactive, and immersive forms of caricature' (2018, 628). Televisual caricature may provide an enticing model for political performance and its parody in this context. However, it is precisely this media environment and its economic and industrial structure that threaten televisual caricature's future sustainability, function and effectiveness.

TV and Caricature has assessed televisual caricature's value as content for a television industry that has undergone significant change over the course of its relatively short life. Most of the televisual caricatures explored in this book, from the scribble, skit, snippet and snatch modes of Chapter 2 to *Spitting Image*, *Fantasy Football League* and *Bo Selecta*, emerged from television as a broadcast medium. Broadcast's structural features, including its temporal specificity, address to an undifferentiated, heterogeneous public, and economic underpinnings either through advertising or public finance, have a significant influence on the form and meaning of televisual caricature in these contexts.

For example, 'snippet' form caricature, in which a comic impersonator embodies their subject as a temporary substitute for the 'real thing', depends on the grammar and discourse of 'ordinary television' (Bonner, 2003), a form that substantially draws on the structuration of the television schedule, the immediacy of live or as-live broadcast and the rhythm of television flow. Televisual caricature's tendency to controversy, either through its critique of social and political elites, or through its deployment of grotesquery and shock, has a commercial expediency in an increasingly competitive television market. It garners attention and prestige and has attracted audiences in demographics that have long been desired by advertisers: young people, those with larger disposable incomes than average (ABC1) and 'light' television viewers, who are harder to reach, and therefore of greater value. Televisual caricature acquired value in the structural, industrial and economic realities of late twentieth-century television.

That *Spitting Image* remains the most obvious example of British televisual caricature speaks to its broadcast at a moment not only of political turbulence, but also at the peak of TV's position at the centre of the cultural public sphere. As a broadcast form, television provided a cultural 'forum' (Newcomb and Hirsch, 1983) through which a citizenry could be addressed simultaneously and immediately. In this context, televisual caricature could play a meaningful role as a humorous reflection of political and social elites, the 'comic public sphere'. Contemporary television's transition away from broadcast towards an on-demand model inevitably limits its ability to shape public perceptions in this way. The likelihood of encountering a mediated caricature that does not flatter pre-existing political affiliation or work within the logic of 'confirmation bias' (Herhuth, 2018) is vastly reduced in a context where our audiovisual content diet is determined by algorithmic recommendation. The on-demand market is also marked by an increasing dependence on content that is detached from a specific time and space. The economics of SVOD services depends on gathering and keeping large numbers of subscribers across multiple territories, such that the localisation generally associated with caricature as a referential art makes it unsuitable transnational content. SVODs' non-linear provision pattern also makes the topicality of caricature a liability where it acted as an asset in a broadcast context. The failure of the *Spitting Image* reboot in the early 2020s demonstrates the precarious future of televisual caricature.

TV and Caricature has presented televisual caricature as a continuation of the tradition of pictorial caricature, visual satire that uses exaggeration, distortion and humour to depict the 'essence' of public figures. Television provides another staging post along this long historical path that has included portraiture, graphic print, newspaper cartooning, animation and cinema. It is logical to suppose that this evolution will continue as moving-image caricature migrates to other media platforms. Indeed, this is already happening with satire online. Nicholas Holm (2023) argues in relation to political humour that the 'professional output' associated with older media, especially television, is now matched by online forms, including political memes and gifs, and emerging outlets such as satirical video and audio podcasts. Holm sees this as evidence of the ongoing health of mediated satire, even as it diminishes as part of 'legacy media':

> … despite the often-predicted end of political satire, the popular appetite for comic comment on politics seems to be showing little sign of slowing even as its expression shifts to better fit the advantages and affordances offered by new media forms. (2023, 83)

Social media sites, especially video-focused ones such as TikTok, Instagram and YouTube, host a huge range of political humour (Davis, Love and Killen, 2018). This includes short-form videos in which comedians, such as Munya Chawawa, Nerine Skinner or Rosie Holt, perform caricatures in skits or parodies. Skinner offers personalised messages from her caricature of former prime minister Liz Truss through the website Cameo. This takes the 'presentational' style of televisual caricature, which creates a playful simulation of direct address between performer and viewer, to its logical endpoint, though dispensing with television as a gatekeeper. As with the 'snippet' caricature (see Chapter 2), the comic impersonation provides an entertaining substitute for the real thing. Online caricatures are often amusingly low-fi, with performers creating surreal physical resemblances to their targets using household objects such as towels or mops in place of wigs or using marker in place of make-up. Just as with televisual caricature, social media caricatures can be light-hearted, gently mocking public personas or employing them parodically as part of a broader political or social commentary. Munya Chawawa's 2020 caricature of Craig David works in this way, a spoof of his song 'Fill Me In' (retitled 'Staying In') that satirises the common experiences shared during the COVID-19 lockdown (Fig. 5.1). Humour is found in the unreality of these impersonations and in their selection of the core features that will connote the identity of the target, in precisely the manner of a caricaturist.

Like most elements of contemporary culture, mediated caricature will surely be irrevocably changed by rapid advances in artificial intelligence. Popular generative AI services such as ChatGPT, Microsoft Copilot or Google Gemini are restricted by their safety features from making portrait caricatures of real people. This is a tacit acknowledgement of caricature's parasitic relationship with existing texts and representations (especially those protected by copyright law), and its potential to cause harm, to defame its targets. AI can, nevertheless, provide

Fig. 5.1 Munya Chawawa performs a parody of Craig David's 'Fill Me In', May 2020

powerful tools for the creation of caricature. The growing sophistication of deepfake technologies – in which AI is used to digitally graft the face of one person onto the body of another – has caused considerable anxiety about the potential for abuse, disinformation and political interference on a large scale. Their dominant use so far has been for the illicit creation of non-consensual pornography (Maddocks, 2022), as visual effects in the film industry (Bode, 2021) and as entertaining experiments that engage the 'curious spectatorship' of fans (Oscar, 2023). In contrast to caricature's antimimetic status, deepfakes promise hyperrealism, radically compromising our ability to trust in the moving image. Deepfakes and caricatures have in common their peculiar interest in the human face as a locus of identity, meaning and value (Bode, Lees and Golding, 2021), as well as their shared practice of 'persona appropriation' (Bode, 2021, 921), the creative (often exaggerated) reuse of physiognomy.

Deepfake videos have already been utilised for caricatural purposes, wherein a celebrity persona becomes a puppet or a mask for a performer to try on and subvert. Perhaps inevitably, Donald Trump has been a commonly satirised figure in this practice. For instance, Trump's face is deployed comically in webseries *Sassy Justice With Fred Sassy* (2021), made by the creators of *South Park*, and featuring deepfake caricatures by impersonator Peter Serafinowicz. Deepfake technology is used in the series, as Graham Meikle points out, 'both as a form of animation and as a form of costuming or make up' (2023, 106). The series parodies American local news presentation via the character of 'Fred Sassy', a reporter tasked with investigating deepfakes. It not only adopts deepfakes as a satirical tool but also comments both on the danger of synthetic media's ability to undermine public trust *and* the hysterical discourse about this new technology in news coverage. 'Sassy' is an invented character, a camp performer who dresses suavely and talks in a nasal, high pitched, lisping voice, but who shares a face with Donald Trump (Fig. 5.2). Though many of the Trump caricature signatures are absent, Sassy still 'calls attention to Trump's highly stylized self-presentation' (Glick, 2023, 104),

Fig. 5.2 Donald Trump transformed into a deepfake caricature in *Sassy Justice With Fred Sassy*, 2020

in an analogous fashion to the televisual caricatures analysed in Chapter 2. Trump also appears 'as himself' in a re-voiced deepfake that, following other mediated Trump caricatures, closely approximates the genuine speech patterns and vocal tics of the president, only exaggerating a little to reveal his absurdity as a political figure. This ironic use of deepfake allows it to share in caricature's use of exaggeration and ridicule as a means of serious critique.

Meikle argues that *Sassy Justice* provides a 'proof of concept for deepfakes as entertainment' (2023, 106), but I would go further to claim that it also shows that deepfakes can be used as an extension of televisual caricature. This potential was realised in 2023, when ITV replaced the *Spitting Image* reboot with the sketch show *Deepfake Neighbour Wars*. This series placed photorealistic impersonations of celebrities in unlikely proximity to one another, creating comedy from the ridiculous conflicts that ensue, and the incongruous distinction between a celebrity persona and everyday behaviour. As Dominic Lees argues, the show demonstrates the creative potential of deepfakes, which can 'can twist and rejuvenate pop culture through their playfulness, while also challenging us to consider what we accept as real' (2023). The capabilities ascribed here to deepfakes apply also to televisual caricatures, which use television form to playfully manipulate popular and political realities, prompting us to reflect, if only momentarily, on the uncomfortable truths that they reveal.

TV and Caricature has traced how televisual caricature is constructed for consumption in the (cultural) public sphere via framing, the address to an implicitly national public with a shared set of references. Online mediated caricature does not operate in this way. The address to the heterogenous coalition of people described as an 'audience' no longer applies, as online caricature is usually circulated within smaller, niche 'micropublics', often politically defined (Marshall, 2014). 'Legacy media', including television, provides clear signals to viewers that what they are seeing and hearing is constructed, humorous and not to be understood literally. In the case of deepfake satire, though, 'such transformations and parodies can more easily reach a viewer as decontextualized fragments' (Ajder and Glick, 2023, 26). The potential danger of such decontextualisation ranges from isolated incidents of misinformation to a wholesale collapse of public trust in images. Drawing from some of the framing and contextualising techniques for mediated caricature discussed in this book might ameliorate these problems, while retaining some of caricature's transgressive pleasures. Considering the matter of framing also highlights what might be lost in the move from televisual to online caricature: the common ground on which television address is built, which it substantially helps to construct, and which supports the function of the comic public sphere. In a political conjuncture marked, as the current one is, by extremes of polarisation, the very idea of such a common ground feels as quaint and nostalgic a construction as an appointment to view the broadcast of a caricature puppet show at 10 p.m. every Sunday evening.

In its focus on televisual caricatures as artefacts of the cultural public sphere, *TV and Caricature* has explored historical changes related to television's address, industries and cultural politics. In its attention to the framing, making and cancelling of televisual caricature, it has suggested a model for the exploration of television texts as their aesthetics, uses, meanings and values change over the course of television history. *TV and Caricature* has provided insight into a televisual context – where 'television' means the quotidian, familiar broadcast device, form and institutions that deliver content of immediate social relevance – that is rapidly disappearing. The transition away from broadcasting has diminished television's expansive mode of address concerned with drawing on common references, shared understandings and agreed-upon knowledges (or at least, knowledge frameworks). There is clearly negative potential in caricature's position as a 'citizenship genre' (Wanzo, 2020). Caricature can police normative moral and social boundaries, resist change or engage in cruelty, offence and stereotype. But televisual caricature also has the capacity to engage a viewer's critical faculties, construct a shared disposition of scepticism to power, to encourage 'silly citizens' (Hartley, 2010) to reflect on social and political values as a key part of the 'comic public sphere' (Caron, 2021). Televisual caricature's future as television content is insecure, since its referentiality compromises its value as content for a global, on-demand media industry. However, the continuing presence of comic impersonations in the digital public sphere offers a glimpse of its legacy.

References

The 11 O'clock Show (1998–2000) [television] Channel 4.
1984: Most Shocking Moments (2024) [television] Channel 5.
2DTV (2001–4) [television] ITV.
30 Rock (2006–13) [television] NBC.
The 80s: Ten Years that Changed Britain (2016) [television] Channel 4.
The 80s With Dominic Sandbrook (2016) [television] BBC Two.
AbsoluteLee Podcast (2022) Jason Lee & David Baddiel Discuss Fantasy Football Blackface Sketches. *AbsoluteLee YouTube Channel*, 21 November. Available from https://www.youtube.com/watch?v=he6Nq2lWLJ0 [accessed 21 February 2024].
Action News (2016) [television] KTNV Channel 13. 19 November 2016, 11.00.
Ajder, H. and Glick, J. (2023) *Just Joking! Deepfakes, Satire and the Politics of Synthetic Media*. Co-Creation Studio / MIT Documentary Lab. Available at https://cocreationstudio.mit.edu/just-joking [accessed 27 February 2025].
Allen, R.C. (1992a) Audience-Oriented Criticism and Television. In: R.C. Allen (ed.) *Channels of Discourse, Reassembled*. Chapel Hill, NC, and London: The University of North Carolina Press, 101–37.
Allen, R.C. (ed.) (1992b) *Channels of Discourse, Reassembled*. Chapel Hill, NC, and London: University of North Carolina Press.
Allen, R.C. and Hill, A. (eds) (2004) *The Television Studies Reader*. London and New York: Routledge.
Anderson, L. (2023) Why So Serious? An Inquiry on Racist Jokes. *Journal of Social Philosophy*, 54(3) 370–84.
Anderson, N. (2022) Spitting Image is CANCELLED after just two seasons. *MailOnline*, 25 October. Available from www.dailymail.co.uk/news/article-11352773/Spitting-Image-CANCELLED-just-two-seasons.html [accessed 31 January 2024].
Andrews, H. (2008) A View from the Demographic: Notes on a Conference. *Screen*, 49(3) 324–30.

Andrews, H. (2019) Distorted Recognition: On the Pleasures of Televisual Historical Caricature. *Screen*, 60(2) 280–97.
Andrews, H. (2020) Drag Celebrity Impersonation as Queer Caricature in the Snatch Game. *Celebrity Studies*, 11(4) 417–30.
Andrews, H. (2025). Transnational Television Caricature: The Global Spread of *Spitting Image* 1984–1994. *Historical Journal of Film, Radio and Television*, 1–21. https://doi.org/10.1080/01439685.2024.2447139.
Andrews, H. and Frame, G. (2025) Cancel Culture: The Decline of Political Comedy on British Television in the Early 2020s. *Comedy Studies*. https://doi.org/10.1080/2040610X.2025.2463773.
Andrews, H. and Sandy-Hindmarch, J. (2024). Content Analysis Data for Project 'Televisual Caricature'. University of Lincoln. Dataset. https://doi.org/10.24385/lincoln.26096386.v1.
Arnheim, R. (1983) The Rationale of Deformation. *Art Journal*, 43(4) 319–24.
Avalon (2021) SPITTING IMAGE RETURNS. *Avalon Press Office*, 1 September. Available from https://avalonuk.com/2021/09/01/spitting-image-returns-september-11-after-record-britbox-uk-subscribers-four-year-record-4-4-million-viewing-figures-for-comedy-on-itv-and-200-milli on-global-views-online/ [accessed 12 March 2024].
Avalon (undated) Spitting Image. *Avalon Distribution*. Available from https://avalon-distribution.com/title/spitting-image [accessed 25 January 2024].
Baddiel and Skinner Unplanned (2000–5) [television] ITV.
Baddiel, D. (2021) *Jews Don't Count: How Identity Politics Failed One Particular Identity*. London: TLS Books.
Bal, A.J., Pitt, L., Berthon, P. and DesAutels, P. (2009) Caricatures, Cartoons, Spoofs and Satires: Political Brands as Butts. *Journal of Public Affairs*, 9 229–37.
BARB (undated a) Most Viewed Programmes, 26 October 2020–1 November 2020. *Broadcasters Audience Research Board*. Available from www.barb.co.uk/viewing-data/most-viewed-programmes [accessed 12 March 2024].
BARB (undated b) *Weekly Top 30 Programmes on TV Sets (July 1998–Sept 2018)*. Available from https://barb.co.uk/viewing-data/weekly-top-30 [accessed 4 March 2024].
Basu, L. (2015) TV Satire and Its Targets: *Have I Got News for You*, *The Thick of It* and *Brass Eye*. In: M. Meijer Drees and S. de Leeuw (eds) *The Power of Satire*. Amsterdam: John Benjamins Publishing Company, 207–15.
Baxter, S. (1991) Thatcher and the Media. *Women: A Cultural Review*, 2(1) 71–3.
BBC News (2019a) Spitting Image show plots return to TV after 23 years. *BBC News*, 28 September. Available from www.bbc.co.uk/news/entertainment-arts-49865406 [accessed 23 January 2024].

BBC News (2019b) BritBox: UK broadcasters enter the streaming wars as new service launches. *BBC News*, 7 November. Available from www.bbc.co.uk/news/entertainment-arts-50320731 [accessed 2 February 2024].

BBC News (2020) Trisha Goddard 'hated' Bo Selecta portrayal. *BBC News*, 12 June. Available from https://www.bbc.co.uk/news/entertainment-arts-53020755 [accessed 4 March 2024].

Becker, A.B. (2020) Trump Trumps Baldwin? How Trump's Tweets Transform SNL into Trump's Strategic Advantage. *Journal of Political Marketing*, 19(4) 386–404.

Becker, A.B. (2021) Alec Baldwin's Appearances on Saturday Night Live: Tangerine Wig, Twitter Backlash, and the Humanising of President Donald J. Trump. *Celebrity Studies*, 12(1) 155–8.

Bedigan, M. (2023) Scrapping episodes of Spitting Image featuring the late Queen cost £9m says ITV. *The Independent*, 21 March. Available from www.independent.co.uk/news/uk/itv-britbox-tom-cruise-boris-johnson-los-angeles-b2304803.html [accessed 31 January 2024].

Benwell, B. (2002) Is There Anything 'New' About These Lads? The Textual and Visual Construction of Masculinity in Men's Magazines. In: L. Litosseliti and J. Sunderland (eds) *Gender Identity and Discourse Analysis*. Amsterdam: John Benjamins Publishing Company, 149–74.

Big Brother (2000–10) [television] Channel 4.

Big Brother's Little Brother (2001–10) [television] E4.

Bignell, J. (2013) *An Introduction to Television Studies* (third edition). London: Routledge.

Billig, M. (2005) Comic Racism and Violence. In: S. Lockyer and M. Pickering (eds) *Beyond a Joke: The Limits of Humour*. Basingstoke: Palgrave, 25–44.

Bishop, T. (1992) Cabinet babes lost in the Euro woods. *The Times*, 16 November, 1.

Black, J. (2020) On Reflexive Racism: Disavowal, Deferment and the Lacanian Subject. *Diacritics*, 48(4) 76–101.

Black, J. (2021) *Race, Racism and Political Correctness in Comedy: A Psychoanalytic Exploration*. London: Routledge.

The Black and White Minstrel Show (1958–78) [television] BBC Television/BBC One.

Blair, J. (2022) *Spitting Image*. Interviewed by H. Andrews, 27 September.

Bloomfield, J. (2023) *Drag: A British History*. Berkeley: University of California Press.

Bo Selecta (2002–4) [television] Channel 4.

Boczkowski, P.J. and Papacharissi, Z. (eds) (2018) *Trump and the Media*. Cambridge, MA, and London: The MIT Press.

Bode, L. (2021) Deepfaking Keanu: YouTube Deepfakes, Platform Visual Effects and the Complexity of Reception. *Convergence*, 27(4) 919–34.

Bode, L., Lees, D. and Golding, D. (2021) The Digital Face and Deepfakes on Screen. *Convergence*, 27(4) 849–54.

BoJack Horseman (2014–20) [streaming television] Netflix.

Bonner, F. (2003) *Ordinary Television*. London: SAGE.

Bonner, P. and Aston, L. (1998) *Independent Television in Britain Vol 5: ITV and the IBA 1981–93: The Old Relationship Changes*. Houndmills and London: Macmillan.

Brand, A.N. (2023) 'What's Wrong with Blackface?' Theorizing Humor Ecologies and Blackface as Satire. *Communication and Critical/Cultural Studies*, 20(2) 215–33.

Brass Eye (1997–2001) [television] Channel 4.

Bremner, Bird and Fortune (1999–2010) [television] Channel 4.

Brennan, N. and Gudelunas, D. (2023) Post-RuPaul's Drag Race: Queer Visibility, Online Discourse and Political Change in a Global Digital Sphere. In: N. Brennan and D. Gudelanas (eds) *Drag in the Global Digital Public Sphere: Queer Visibility, Online Discourse and Political Change*. London: Routledge, 1–13.

Brillenburg Wurth, K. (2011) Spitting Image and Pre-Televisual Political Satire: Graphics and Puppets to Screens. *Image & Narrative*, 12(3) 113–36.

Brown, M. (2007) *A Licence to Be Different: The Story of Channel 4*. London: BFI.

Bucaria, C. and Barra, L. (2016) Taboo Comedy on Television: Issues and Themes. In: C. Bucharia and L. Barra (eds) *Taboo Comedy: Television and Controversial Humour*. Basingstoke: Palgrave, 1–18.

Butler, J. (1990). *Gender Trouble: Feminism and the Subversion of Identity*. London: Routledge.

Cammaerts, B. (2022) The Abnormalisation of Social Justice: The 'Anti-Woke Culture War' Discourse in the UK. *Discourse & Society*, 33(6) 730–43.

Caron, J. (2021) *Satire as the Comic Public Sphere: Postmodern Truthiness and Civic Engagement*. Philadelphia: Penn State University Press.

Carroll, N. (2014) *Humour: A Very Short Introduction*. Oxford: Oxford University Press.

Casey, B., Casey, N., Calvert, B., French, L. and Lewis, J. (2008) *Television Studies: The Key Concepts* (second edition). London: Routledge.

Central Television (1986) Central Television: A model for the future. *The Times*, 3 November, 33.

Chalaby, J.K. (2016) *The Format Age: Television's Entertainment Revolution*. London: Polity.

Channel 4 (2003) *Channel Four Television Corporation Report and Financial Statements 2003*. Available from https://assets-corporate.channel4.com/_flysystem/s3/2017-06/annual_report_2003.pdf [accessed 4 March 2024].
Channel 4 (undated) *Equity & Inclusion*. Available from: www.channel4.com/corporate/about-4/operating-responsibly/diversity. [accessed 12 February 2025].
Chester, L. (1986) *Tooth & Claw: The Inside Story of Spitting Image*. London: Faber & Faber.
Coleman, B. (2007) Thatcher the gay icon. *The New Statesman*, 25 June. Available from www.newstatesman.com/politics/2007/06/lady-thatcher-gay-tory [accessed 2 February 2024].
Condren, C. (2012) Satire and Definition. *Humor*, 25(4) 375–99.
Connerton, P. (2008) Seven Types of Forgetting. *Memory Studies*, 1(1) 59–71.
Corner, J. (1995) *Television Form and Public Address*. London and New York: Edward Arnold.
Crossroads (1964–88) [television] ITV.
Curran, J. (1991) Rethinking the Media as a Public Sphere. In: P. Dahlgren and C. Sparks (eds) *Communication and Citizenship: Journalism and the Public Sphere in the New Media Age*. London: Routledge, 27–57.
Curry and Chips (1969) [television] ITV.
Custis, N. (1996) Pinapple: I'll run rings round them. LEE'S top of the crops. *The Sun*, 24 July, 30.
Cutting Edge: Footballers' Wives (1997) [television] Channel 4. 11 November 1997, 21.00.
Da Ali G Show (2000–4) [television] Channel 4.
Dahlgren, P. (1995) *Television and the Public Sphere: Citizenship, Democracy and the Media*. London: Sage.
Darlow, M. (2004) *Independents Struggle: The Programme Makers Who Took on the TV Establishment*. London: Quartet.
David Baddiel: Jews Don't Count (2022) [television] Channel 4. 21 November 2022, 21.00.
David, C. (2022) *What's Your Vibe? Tuning Into Your Best Life*. London: Penguin.
Davies, C. (2016) The Rise and Fall of Taboo Comedy in the BBC. In: C. Bucaria and L. Barra (eds) *Taboo Comedy: Television and Controversial Humour*. Basingstoke: Palgrave, 21–40.
Davies, H.C. and MacRae, S.E. (2023) An Anatomy of the British War on Woke. *Race & Class*, 65(2) 3–54.
Davis, J.L., Love, T.P. and Killen, G. (2018) Seriously Funny: The Political Work of Humor on Social Media. *new media & society*, 20(10) 3898–3916.
de Kosnik, A. (2016) *Rogue Archives: Digital Cultural Memory and Media Fandom*. Cambridge, MA: University of Massachusetts Press.

Dead Ringers (2002–7) [television] BBC Two.
Declercq, D. (2018) A Definition of Satire (And Why a Definition Matters). *Journal of Aesthetics and Art Criticism*, 76(3) 319–30.
Deepfake Neighbour Wars (2023–) [television] ITV.
Delaney, S. (2006) 'We're just mucking about'. *The Guardian*, 11 October. Available from www.theguardian.com/stage/2006/oct/11/comedy [accessed 13 March 2024].
Delingpole, J. (2020) Has Spitting Image ever been funny? *The Spectator*, 31 October. Available from www.spectator.co.uk/article/has-spitting-image-ever-been-funny [accessed 31 January 2024].
Denton, C. (1984) *Letter From to IBA Director of Television Dated 29th February 1984* (unpublished). IBA Archive, Box 3996159, File 5081/2/93. Bournemouth: Bournemouth University Library.
Denton, C. (2023) *Spitting Image*. Interviewed by H. Andrews, 12 February.
Donald, D. (1996) *The Age of Caricature: Satirical Prints in the Reign of George III*. New Haven, CT, and London: Yale University Press.
Drunk History UK (2015–7) [television] Comedy Central UK.
Dugdale, J. (1990) Laughing Stocks. *The Listener*, 1 November, 15.
Duguid, M. (undated) Race and the Sitcom. *BFI Screenonline*. Available from http://www.screenonline.org.uk/tv/id/1108234/index.html [accessed 1 March 2024].
Eagleton, T. (2019) *Humour*. New Haven, CT, and London: Yale University Press.
Edwards, J. and Graulund, R. (2013) *The Grotesque*. London and New York: Routledge.
Ellis, J. (1992) *Visible Fictions: Cinema Television Video*. London: Routledge.
Fantasy Football League (1994–6) [television] BBC Two.
Farr, M. (2018) *Spitting Image*: The puppet satire that captured Thatcher's Britain. *The Conversation*, 23 November. Available from https://theconversation.com/spitting-image-the-puppet-satire-that-captured-thatchers-britain-107241 [accessed 30 January 2024].
Feaver, W. (1981) *Masters of Caricature: From Hogarth and Gillray to Scarfe and Levine*. London: Weidenfeld and Nicolson.
Ferris, K. and Harris, S.R. (2011) *Stargazing: Celebrity, Fame and Social Interaction*. New York and London: Routledge.
Fluck, P. (2022) *Spitting Image*. Interviewed by H. Andrews, 8 July.
Flynn, P.P. (2006) Margaret Thatcher: Gay icon. *The Guardian*, 16 May. Available from www.theguardian.com/commentisfree/2006/may/16/bypaulflynn [accessed 2 February 2024].
Framke, C. (2020) Why removing blackface episodes is 'just trying to band-aid over history'. *Variety*, 1 July. Available from https://variety.com/2020/

tv/news/blackface-episodes-pulled-30-rock-golden-girls-community-1234694796 [accessed 4 March 2024].

Fraser, N. (1992) Rethinking the Public Sphere: A Contribution to the Critique of Actually Existing Democracy. In C.J. Calhoun (ed.) *Habermas and the Public Sphere*. Cambridge, MA: MIT Press, 109–42.

Frean, A. (1996) Last stretch for rubber stars who miss Iron Lady. *The Times*, 13 January, 8.

Freud, S. (1976) *Jokes and Their Relation to the Unconscious* (trans. James Strachey). Harmondsworth: Penguin.

Futurama (1999–) [television] Fox/Comedy Central/Hulu.

Garnham, N. (1992) The Media and the Public Sphere. In: C. Calhoun. (ed.) *Habermas and the Public Sphere*. London: MIT Press, 359–76.

Geraghty, C. and Lusted, D. (eds) (1997) *The Television Studies Book*. London: Arnold.

Gilbert, C.J. (2021) *Argumentum ad Carricare* as a Mode of Character Attack: Alec Baldwin as Donald Trump on Saturday Night Live. In: S.A. Samoilenko, M. Icks, J. Keohane and E. Shiraev (eds) *Routledge Handbook of Character Assassination and Reputation Management*. London and New York: Routledge, 209–24.

Gill, R. (2003) Power and the Production of Subjects: A Genealogy of the New Man and the New Lad. *The Sociological Review*, 51(1) 34–56.

Glick, J. (2023) Deepfake Satire and the Possibilities of Synthetic Media. *Afterimage* 50(3) 81–107.

Godfrey, S. (2022) *Masculinity in British Cinema: 1990–2010*. Edinburgh: Edinburgh University Press.

Goldstraw, S. (2023) 'It Was Just a Joke!' Comedy and Freedom of Speech. *European Journal of Political Theory*. Available from https://doi.org/10.1177/14748851231205375 [accessed 4 March 2024].

Gombrich, E.H. (2002) *Art and Illusion: A Study in the Psychology of Pictorial Representation* (sixth edition). London: Phaidon.

Gombrich, E.H. and Kris, E. (1938) The Principles of Caricature. *British Journal of Medical Psychology*, 17 319–42.

Gombrich, E.H. and Kris, E. (1940) *Caricature*. Harmondsworth: King Penguin.

Gone with the Wind (1939) Dir. Victor Fleming, Loew's Inc.

Good Morning Britain (1985) TV AM. 13 April 1985, 07.50.

Gorton, K. and Garde-Hansen, J. (2019) *Remembering British Television: Audience, Archive and Industry*. London: BFI.

Grandy, C. (2020) 'The Show is Not About Race': Custom, Screen Culture, and the Black and White Minstrel Show. *Journal of British Studies*, 59(4) 857–84.

Gray, J. and Lotz, A.D. (2019) *Television Studies* (second edition). Cambridge and Malden, MA: Polity.

Gray, J., Jones, J. and Thompson, E. (2009) The State of Satire, the Satire of State. In: J. Gray J. Jones and E. Thompson (eds) *Satire TV: Politics and Comedy in the Post-Network Era*. New York: NYU Press, 3–36.

Graye, M. (2022) Leigh Francis says Craig David needs to 'move on' from Bo Selecta row. *The Independent*, 23 November. Available from www.independent.co.uk/arts-entertainment/tv/news/keith-lemon-craig-david-bo-selecta-b2231185.html [accessed 4 March 2024].

Green Wing (2004–7) [television] Channel 4.

Greenberg, J. (2018) *The Cambridge Introduction to Satire*. Cambridge: Cambridge University Press.

Griffin, D. (1994) *Satire: A Critical Reintroduction*. Lexington: University Press of Kentucky.

The Guardian (1999) Thatcher's Legacy. *The Guardian*, 3 May. Available from www.theguardian.com/politics/1999/may/03/thatcher.uk [accessed 20 January 2023].

Les guignols de l'info (1988–2018) [television] Canal+.

Habermas, J. (1992) *The Structural Transformation of the Public Sphere: An Enquiry into a Category of Bourgeois Society* (trans. Thomas Burger). Cambridge: Polity.

Hadley, L. and Ho, E. (eds) (2010) *Thatcher and After: Margaret Thatcher and Her Afterlife in Contemporary Culture*. Basingstoke: Palgrave Macmillan.

Hall, S. (2007) Encoding/Decoding in the Television Discourse. In A. Gray, J. Campbell, M. Erickson, S. Hanson and H. Wood (eds) *CCCS Selected Working Papers* (Volume 2), 386–98.

Harmes, M.K. (2013) A Creature Not Quite of This World: Adaptations of Margaret Thatcher on 1980s British Television. *Journal of Popular Television*, 1(1) 53–68.

Hartley, J. (2010) Silly Citizenship. *Critical Discourse Studies*, 7(4) 233–48.

Hartley, J. and Green, J. (2006) The Public Sphere on the Beach. *European Journal of Cultural Studies*, 9(5) 341–62.

Headcases (2008) [television] ITV.

Hendy, D. (2022) The Black and White Minstrel Show. *History of the BBC*. Available from www.bbc.com/historyofthebbc/100-voices/people-nation-empire/make-yourself-at-home/the-black-and-white-minstrel-show [accessed 15 February 2024].

Herhuth, E. (2018) Overloading, Incongruity, Animation: A Theory of Caricature and Caricatural Logic in Contemporary Media. *Theory & Event*, 21(3), 627–51.

Herr, O. (2020) Don't Show and Tell. *Index on Censorship*, 49(3) 22–3.

Hill Collins, P. (2022) *Black Feminist Thought: Knowledge, Consciousness and the Politics of Empowerment* (30th anniversary edition). London: Routledge.

Hilmes, M. (1985) The Televisual Apparatus: Direct Address. *Journal of Film and Video*, 37(4) 27–36.

Hislop, I. (1988) Spitting back. *Daily Telegraph*, 8 December, 14.

Hodges, M. (2021) Mocking the afflicted: For the Spitting Image team, pompous celebrities – and RT writers – get what's coming to them. But is anyone off limits? *Radio Times*, 7 September, 24–5.

Holm, N. (2023) The Limits of Satire, or the Reification of Cultural Politics. *Thesis Eleven*, 174(1) 81–97.

Horrible Histories (2009–24) [television] CBBC.

Hoskins, C. McFadyen, S. and Finn, A. (2004) *Media Economics: Applying Economics to New and Traditional Media*. Thousand Oaks, CA: SAGE Publications.

Howell, W. and Parry-Giles, T. (2018) 'I'm About to Be President: We're All Going to Die': Baldwin, Trump and the Rhetorical Power of Comedic Presidential Impersonation. In: B.R. Warner, D.G. Bystrom, M.S. McKinney and M.C. Banwart (eds) *An Unprecedented Election: Media, Communication and the Electorate in the 2016 Campaign*. Santa Barbara, CA: Prager, 151–66.

Howitt, D. and Owusu-Bempah, K. (2005) Race and Ethnicity in Popular Humour. In: S. Lockyer and M. Pickering (eds) *Beyond a Joke: The Limits of Humour*. Basingstoke: Palgrave, 45–62.

Hunt, L. (2013) *Cult British TV Comedy: From Reeves and Mortimer to Psychoville*. Manchester: Manchester University Press.

Hutcheon, L. (1994) *Irony's Edge: The Theory and Politics of Irony*. London: Routledge.

Hutcheon, L. (2000) *A Theory of Parody: The Teachings of Twentieth Century Art Forms*. Urbana and Chicago: University of Illinois Press.

IBA (1984a) *Letter from IBA Programme Officer to Chairman, Dated 17 January 1984* (unpublished). IBA Archive, Archive box 3996159 File 5081/2/93: Central Programmes 'Spitting Image' Feb 1984–Oct 1986 Vol. 1. Bournemouth: Bournemouth University Library.

IBA (1984b) *Letter From IBA Officer to Member of the Public, Dated 8 March 1984* (unpublished). IBA Archive, Box 3996159, File 5081/2/93: Central Programmes 'Spitting Image' Feb 1984–Oct 1986 Vol. 1. Bournemouth: Bournemouth University Library.

IBA (1985) *Extract From Minutes of the 600th Meeting of the IBA, Dated 16th January 1985* (unpublished). IBA Archive, Box 3996159, File 5081/2/93: Central Programmes 'Spitting Image' Feb 1984–Oct 1986 Vol. 1. Bournemouth: Bournemouth University Library.

IBA (1986a) *Letter From Deputy Director of Television to IBA Monitor, Dated 3 February 1986*. IBA Archive, Box 3996159, File 5081/2/93: Central Programmes 'Spitting Image' Feb 1984–Oct 1986 Vol. 1. Bournemouth: Bournemouth University Library.

IBA (1986b) *Letter From IBA Regional Officer to IBA Monitor, Dated 30 January 1986*. IBA Archive, Box 3996159, File 5081/2/93: Central Programmes 'Spitting Image' Feb 1984–Oct 1986 Vol. 1. Bournemouth: Bournemouth University Library.

IBA (1987) *Letter From Director General of the IBA to Complainant, Dated 4 November 1987* (unpublished). IBA Archive, Box 3996159, File 5081/2/93: Central Programmes 'Spitting Image' Nov 1986–Dec 1988 Vol. 2. Bournemouth: Bournemouth University Library.

Iley, C. (2009) 'I'm just not very good at being me': Time out Leigh Francis. *The Times* (weekend supplement), 12 September, 4–5.

The Imitation Game (2018) [television] ITV.

The Impressions Show (2009–11) [television] BBC One.

ITV News (2014) 30 Facts for 30 Years – The truth about Spitting Image. *ITV News*, 26 February. Available from www.itv.com/news/central/2014-02-26/30-facts-for-30-years-the-truth-about-spitting-image [accessed 23 January 2024].

ITV PLC (2021) *ITV: More than TV: ITV PLC Annual Report and Accounts for the Year Ended 31 December 2020*. Available from https://www.itvplc.com/~/media/Files/I/ITV-PLC-V2/documents/investors/result-centre/reports-and-results/annual-report-2020.pdf [accessed 31 January 2024].

ITV PLC (2022) *Digital Acceleration: Phase Two of ITV's More than TV strategy: ITV PLC Annual Report and Accounts for the Year Ended 31 December 2021*. Available from www.itvplc.com/~/media/Files/I/ITV-PLC/documents/reports-and-results/annual-report-2021.pdf [accessed 31 January 2024].

ITV PLC (2023) *Strategic EXECUTION: ITV PLC Annual Report and Accounts for the Year Ended 31 December 2022*. Available from www.itvplc.com/~/media/Files/I/ITV-PLC/documents/reports-and-results/annual-result-2022-v2.pdf [accessed 31 January 2024].

ITV Press Office (2020) Britbox announces critically acclaimed iconic British satire show, *Spitting Image*, to return in Autumn 2021. *ITV*, 7 October. Available from www.itv.com/presscentre/britbox/media-releases/britbox-announces-critically-acclaimed-iconic-british-satire-show-spitting-image [accessed 26 January 2024].

Janes, D. (2012) 'One of Us': The Queer Afterlife of Margaret Thatcher as a Gay Icon. *International Journal of Media & Cultural Politics*, 8(2–3) 211–27.

Jenner, M. (2016) Is This TVIV? On Netflix, TVIII and Binge-Watching. *new media & society*, 18(2) 257–73.

Jenner, M. (2018) *Netflix and the Re-Invention of Television*. Cham: Palgrave.

Johnson, S. (2012) *Burnt Cork: Traditions and Legacies of Blackface Minstrelsy*. Amherst: University of Massachusetts Press.

Jones, J. (2015) The Authenticity of Play: Satiric Television's Challenge to Authoritative Discourses. In: M. Meijer Drees and S. de Leeuw (eds) *The Power of Satire*. Amsterdam: John Benjamins Publishing Company, 33–46.

Jones, J.P. (2013) Politics and the Brand: *Saturday Night Live*'s Campaign Season Humor. In: N. Marx, M. Sienkiewicz and R. Becker (eds) *Saturday Night Live and American TV*. Bloomington: Indiana University Press, 77–92.

Jonze, T. (2022) 'There's never been a time when you could just say anything': Frank Skinner on free speech, his bullying shame – and knob jokes. *The Guardian*, 25 July. Available from www.theguardian.com/stage/2022/jul/25/frank-skinner-standup-comic-free-speech-poetry-comedy-lad dish-image [accessed 21 February 2024].

Joseph, J. (1996) Thatch of the day. *The Times*, 8 June, 29 [S3].

Joyce, H. (2010) Parodic Reiterations: Representations of Margaret Thatcher and Thatcherism in Late Twentieth-Century British Political Cartoons. In: L. Hadley and E. Ho (eds) *Thatcher and After: Margaret Thatcher and Her Afterlife in Contemporary Culture*. Basingstoke: Palgrave Macmillan, 221–43.

Kanai, A. and Gill, R. (2021) Woke? Affect, Neoliberalism, Marginalised Identities and Consumer Culture. *new formations* 102, 10–27.

Kant, I. (1914) *Critique of Judgement* (trans. J.H. Bernard). London: Macmillan.

Kellner, D. (2016) *American Nightmare: Donald Trump, Media Spectacle and Authoritarian Populism*. Rotterdam, Boston and Taipei: Sense Publishers.

Kemp, E. (2020) 'Spitting Image' defends depiction of Greta Thunberg after social media criticism. *NME*, 30 September. Available from https://www.nme.com/news/tv/spitting-image-defends-depiction-of-greta-thun berg-after-social-media-backlash-2765611 [accessed 31 January 2024].

Knight, H. (1986) 20 things you never knew about zany Spitting Image! *The Sun*, 13 January, 9.

Krefting, R. and Baruc, R. (2015) A New Economy of Jokes? #Socialmedia #comedy. *Comedy Studies*, 6(2) 129–40.

Kuipers, G. (2015) Satire and Dignity. In: M. Meijer Drees and S. de Leeuw (eds) *The Power of Satire*. Amsterdam: John Benjamins Publishing Company, 19–32.

Kuś, R. (2022) *Our Cartoon President*: Donald J. Trump's White House as an Animated Comedy. In: K. McNally (ed.) *American Television During a Television Presidency*. Detroit, MI: Wayne State University Press, 35–50.

The Late Show With Stephen Colbert (2015–) [television] CBS.
Law, R. (1994) *Fax to Richard Bennett and Steve Bendelack, Dated 19 March 1994*. Roger Law Collection, File: Add.10275/4/52 Franchise Documentary 1983–1997. Cambridge, Cambridge University Library.
Law, R. (1997) One Genuinely University Bit of Mischief. In: The Centre for the Study of Cartoons and Caricature, University of Kent (ed.) *A Sense of Permanence? Essays on the Art of the Cartoon*. London: Park McDonald, 45–52.
Law, R. (2022) *Spitting Image*. Interviewed by H. Andrews, 20 May.
Law, R., Chester, L. and Evans, A. (1992) *A Nasty Piece of Work: The Art and Graft of Spitting Image*. London: Internos Books.
Lawson, M. (2020) Spitting Image review – welcome return for comedy that revels in giving offence. *The Guardian*, 3 October. Available from www.theguardian.com/tv-and-radio/2020/oct/03/spitting-image-review-welcome-return-for-comedy-that-revels-in-giving-offence [accessed 31 January 2024].
Lees, D. (2023) *Deep Fake Neighbour Wars*: ITV's comedy shows how AI can transform popular culture. *The Conversation*, 27 January. Available at https://theconversation.com/deep-fake-neighbour-wars-itvs-comedy-shows-how-ai-can-transform-popular-culture-198569 [accessed 4 June 2024].
Leith, L. (2023) David Baddiel: Football fills a God shaped hole. *The Guardian*, 18 March. Available from www.theguardian.com/books/2023/mar/18/david-baddiel-football-fills-a-god-shaped-hole [accessed 4 March 2024].
Lewis, M.B. and Johnston, R.A. (1998) Understanding Caricatures of Faces. *The Quarterly Journal of Experimental Psychology*, 51(2) 321–46.
Little Britain (2003–6) [television] BBC Three/BBC One.
Littleton, C. (2015) FX Networks Chief John Landgraf: 'There Is Simply Too Much Television'. *Variety*, 7 August. Available from https://variety.com/2015/tv/news/tca-fx-networks-john-landgraf-wall-street-1201559191 [accessed 22 January 2024].
Lloyd, J. (2022) *Spitting Image*. Interviewed by H. Andrews, 6 May.
London Standard (1988) Waxworks to make you spit. *London Standard*, 8 February, 3.
London Underground (1993) This weekend, dance around London by Tube. *Richmond & Twickenham Informer*, 28 May, 23.
Lotz, A.D. (2017) *Portals: A Treatise on Internet-Distributed Television*. Ann Arbor, MI: Maize.
Lotz, A.D. and Eklund, O. (2024) Beyond Netflix: Ownership and Content Strategies Among Non-US-Based Streaming Services. *International Journal of Cultural Studies*, 27(1) 119–40.

Lotz, A.D., Potter, A. and Johnson, C. (2021) Understanding the Changing Television Market: A Comparison of the Macroeconomy of the United States, United Kingdom and Australia. *Convergence*, 28(1) 272–90.

Low, V. (1996) The fantasy farce: Pineapple player up for sale after BBC TV show made him the butt of fans' jokes. *Evening Standard*, 22 May, 3.

Lucie-Smith, E. (1981) *The Art of Caricature*. London: Orbis Publishing.

Lury, K. (2005) *Interpreting Television*. London and New York: Bloomsbury.

Lury, K. (2011) 'The Basis for Mutual Contempt': The Loss of the Contingent in Digital Television. In Bennett, J. and Strange, N. (eds) *Television as Digital Media*. Durham, NC: Duke University Press, 181–203.

Maddocks, S (2020) 'A Deepfake Porn Plot Intended to Silence Me': Exploring Continuities Between Pornographic and 'Political' Deep Fakes. *Porn Studies*, 7(4) 415–23.

Maggie & Me (2013) [television] Channel 4, 8 April 2013.

Malik, N. (2020) The return of Spitting Image shows how toothless British satire has become. *The Guardian*, 11 October. Available from www.theguardian.com/commentisfree/2020/oct/11/spitting-image-british-satire-powerful [accessed 31 January 2024].

Malik, S. (2008) 'Keeping It Real': The Politics of Channel 4's Multiculturalism, Mainstreaming and Mandates. *Screen*, 49(3) 343–53.

Margaret Thatcher: Where Am I Now? (1999) [television] Channel 4, 26–30 April.

Marshall, P.D. (2014) Persona Studies: Mapping the Proliferation of the Public Self. *Journalism*, 15(2) 153–70.

The Mary Whitehouse Experience (1991–2) [television] BBC Two.

The Match Game (1962–) [television] NBC/CBS/ABC/Syndication.

Mauro, R. and Kubovy, M. (1992) Caricature and Face Recognition. *Memory and Cognition*, 20(4) 433–40.

Maxwell, D. (2020) The new Spitting Image shows politics is still a laughing matter. *The Times*, 3 October, 19.

McElwee, M. (1999) The Thatcher legacy. *BBC News*, 28 April. Available from http://news.bbc.co.uk/1/hi/special_report/1999/04/99/thatcher_anniversary/330546.stm [accessed 20 January 2023].

McGuigan, J. (2002) *Culture and the Public Sphere*. London: Routledge.

McGuigan, J. (2005) The Cultural Public Sphere. *European Journal of Cultural Studies*, 8(4) 427–43.

McGuigan, J. (2011) The Cultural Public Sphere – A Critical Measure of Public Culture? In: G. Delanty, L. Giorgi and M. Sassatelli (eds) *Festivals and the Cultural Public Sphere*. London: Routledge, 79–91.

McPhee, R. (2021) The latex news upset [sic] wokes … SPITTING IMAGE TONES DOWN SHOW. *The Sun*, 29 July 2021, 31.

Media Archive for Central England (undated) *Central News East: 02.03.1984: Duke of Edinburgh Opens Lenton Lane Studio*. Available from www.macearchive.org/films/central-news-east-02031984-duke-edinburgh-opens-lenton-lane-studio [accessed 10 January 2024].

Meikle, G. (2023) *Deepfakes*. London: Polity.

Meinhof, U. and J. Smith (2000) Spitting Image: TV Genre and Intertextuality. In: U. Meinhof and J. Smith (eds) *Intertextuality and the Media: From Genre to Everyday Life*. Manchester: Manchester University Press, 43–60.

Melaniphy, M. (1984) *Television & Radio 1985: Guide to Independent Broadcasting*. London: IBA.

Melaniphy, M. (1985) *Television & Radio 1986: Yearbook of Independent Broadcasting*. London: IBA.

The Melting Pot (1975) [television] BBC One.

Michalis, M. (2022) Public Service Broadcasting in the Online Television Environment: The Case for PSB VoD Players and the Role of Policy Focusing on the BBC iPlayer. *International Journal of Communication*, 16 525–44.

Mills, B. (2009) *The Sitcom*. Edinburgh: Edinburgh University Press.

Mills, B. (2016) A Special Freedom: Regulating Comedy Offence. In: C. Bucaria and L. Barra (eds) *Taboo Comedy: Television and Controversial Humour*. Basingstoke: Palgrave, 209–26.

Moir, J. (2020) FIRST REVIEW: It's no joke – Spitting Image's new marvels of boneless spite are let down by lame scripts. *MailOnline*, 2 October. Available from www.dailymail.co.uk/tvshowbiz/article-8799843/JAN-MOIR-reviews-Spitting-Image.html [accessed 31 January 2024].

Mondal, A.A. (2018) Taking Liberties? Free Speech, Multiculturalism and the Ethics of Satire. In: H. Davies and S. Ilott (eds) *Comedy and the Politics of Representation*. Cham: Palgrave Macmillan, 25–41.

Moore, M. (2020) America runs scared of *Spitting Image*. *The Times*, 7 October. Available from www.thetimes.co.uk/article/america-runs-scared-of-spitting-image-zxjx2j6x2 [accessed 29 January 2024].

Moran, A. (2013) Global Television Formats: Genesis and Growth. *Critical Studies in Television*, 8(2) 1–19.

Morris, R.N. (1995) *The Carnivalization of Politics: Quebec Cartoons on Relations with Canada, England, and France, 1960–1979*. Montreal and London: McGill University Press.

Murray, M. (2022) The Imaginary President: Donald Trump's Narcissism and American TV. In K. McNally (ed.) *American Television During a Television Presidency*. Detroit, MI: Wayne State University Press, 19–35.

Nallon, S. (2022) *Spitting Image*. Interviewed by H. Andrews, 30 June.

Naylor, D. (2022) *Spitting Image*. Interviewed by H. Andrews, 6 October.

Newcomb, H. and Hirsch, P. (1983) Television as Cultural Forum: Implications for Research. *Quarterly Review of Film and Video*, 8(3) 45–55.

Newman, N. (2023) Puppet politics: Is this Spitting Image's final bow? *The Sunday Times*, 26 February, 9.

Newzoids (2015–16) [television] ITV.

Ng, E. (2022) *Cancel Culture: A Critical Analysis*. Cham: Palgrave.

Not the Nine O'clock News (1979–82) [television] BBC One.

Nunn, H. (2002) *Thatcher, Politics and Fantasy: The Political Culture of Gender and Nation*. London: Lawrence & Wishart.

O'Grady, S. (2020) Spitting Image election specials review: Running true to its visually splendid form. *The Independent*, 31 October. Available from www.independent.co.uk/arts-entertainment/tv/reviews/spitting-image-review-b1481978.html [accessed 31 January 2024].

O'Malley, T. and Jones, J. (eds) (2009) *The Peacock Committee and UK Broadcasting Policy*. Basingstoke: Palgrave Macmillan.

Odumosu, T. (2017) *Africans in English Caricature 1769–1819: Black Jokes, White Humour*. London: Harvey Miller.

Ofcom (2022) Media Nations Report 2022. *Ofcom*, 17 August. Available from www.ofcom.org.uk/data/assets/pdf_file/0016/242701/media-nations-report-2022.pdf [accessed 31 January 2024].

Oliver and Ohlbaum (2020) Why securing platform carriage deals is vital for BritBox. *Oliver & Ohlbaum*, 2 March. Available from www.oando.co.uk/insight/britbox [accessed 25 January 2024].

Omnibus: Luck & Flaw's Illustrated Guide to Caricature (1985) [television] BBC One, 26 July, 22.15.

Oscar, S. (2023) Curious Spectatorship in the Age of Deepfakes. *Digital Creativity*, 34(3) 230–47.

Osur, S. (2022) #WokeTV Beyond the Hashtag: *One Day at a Time* and *The Baby-Sitters Club* as Woke Classic Television. *Journal of Popular Film and Television*, 50(2) 69–79.

Our Cartoon President (2018–20) [television] Showtime.

Patrick, H. (2024) Former Thatcher adviser quotes Spitting Image sketch as fact in live interview. *The Independent*, 21 March. Available at www.independent.co.uk/tv/news/margaret-thatcher-spitting-image-gb-news-b2516316.html [accessed 30 January 2025].

Pelley, R. (2020) 'The more complaints we got, the better' – How Spitting Image redefined satire. *The Guardian*, 1 October. Available from www.theguardian.com/tv-and-radio/2020/oct/01/spitting-image-satire-ian-hislop-roy-hattersley [accessed 23 January 2024].

Pérez, R. (2021) *The Souls of White Jokes: How Racist Humor Fuels White Supremacy*. Redwood, CA: Stanford University Press.

Peters, L. and Becker, S. (2010) Racism in Comedy Reappraised: Back to Little England? *Comedy Studies*, 1(2) 191–200.
Pickering, M. (2001) *Stereotyping: The Politics of Representation*. Basingstoke: Palgrave.
Pickering, M. (2008) *Blackface Minstrelsy in Britain*. Aldershot: Ashgate.
Poniewozik, J. (2019) *Audience of One: Donald Trump, Television and the Fracturing of America*. New York: Liveright.
Potter, I. (2008) *The Rise and Rise of The Independents: A Television History*. London: Guerilla Books.
Prior, M. (2007) *Post-Broadcast Democracy: How Media Choice Increases Inequality in Political Involvement and Polarizes Elections*. Cambridge: Cambridge University Press.
Psychobitches (2013–14) [television] Sky Arts.
Ravens, J. (2022) *Spitting Image*. Interviewed by H. Andrews, 21 October.
Reade, B. (2020) Political muppets are such a hopeless joke that they're beyond satire. *The Mirror*, 2 October. Available from www.mirror.co.uk/news/politics/brian-reade-political-muppets-hopeless-22783063 [accessed 31 January 2024].
Rhodes, G. (1996) *Superportraits: Caricatures and Recognition*. Hove: The Psychology Press.
Robbins, K. (2022) *Spitting Image*. Interviewed by H. Andrews, 8 November.
Rory Bremner, Who Else (1993–8) [television] Channel 4.
Ross, E. (2006) The Representation of Immigrants and Immigration in UK Political Cartoons From 1968 to 2005. *The International Journal of Comic Art*, 8(2) 283–306.
Rota, O. (1987) Novelas, satira e rock gli assi di Montecarlo [Novelas, satire and rock the aces of Montecarlo]. *La Stampa*, 17 September, 22.
Royal Television Society (2021) Production Focus: Spitting Image. *Royal Television Society*, 22 July. Available from https://rts.org.uk/event/spitting-image-production-focus [accessed 29 January 2024].
RuPaul's Drag Race UK (2019–) [television] BBC Three.
Saha, A. (2020) The Politics of Representation in the Politics of Anti-racism. *Ethnic and Racial Studies*, 43(13) 2357–62.
Sassy Justice with Fred Sassy (2021) [webseries] YouTube.
Saturday Night Live (1975–) [television] NBC.
Scarlata, A. and Lynch, A. (2023) Opting Out of the Streaming Wars: Second and Third Tier SVODS. In: C.Adamou and S.Petridis (eds) *Television by Stream: Essays on Marketing, Content and Audience Worldwide*. Jefferson, NC: McFarland, 95–110.
Scrubs (2001–10) [television] NBC/ABC.

Scully, E. (2020) British satirical show Spitting Image is hit by anti-Semitism storm after puppet of Facebook founder Mark Zuckerberg is given a large nose and 'ghoulish appearance'. *MailOnline*, 15 September. Available from www.dailymail.co.uk/news/article-8734635/Spitting-Image-hit-anti-Semitism-storm-puppet-Mark-Zuckerberg-given-large-nose.html [accessed 31 January 2024].

Seymour-Ure, C. (2003) *Prime Ministers and the Media: Issues of Power and Control*. London: Wiley.

Sheehan, P. (1996) Lee: It is not funny. *The Sun*, 23 May, 50.

Sherry, J. (1987) Four Modes of Caricature: Reflections Upon a Genre. *Bulletin of Research in the Humanities*, 87(1) 29–62.

The Silence of the Lambs (1991) Dir. Jonathan Demme, Orion Pictures.

The Simpsons (1989–) [television] Fox.

Singh, A. (2020) Cabinet's lack of characters and too many pulled punches make for a less edifying Image. *Daily Telegraph*, 3 October, 13.

Sobande, F. Kanai, A. and Zeng, N. (2022) The Hypervisibility and Discourses of 'Wokeness' in Digital Culture. *Media, Culture & Society*, 44(8) 1576–87.

South Park (1997–) [television] Comedy Central.

Spit 'n' Image Productions (1982) *Spit' N' Image Proposal* (unpublished). Roger Law Collection, File: GBR/0012/MS Add.10275/4/32. Cambridge: Cambridge University Library.

Spitting Image (1984–96) [television] ITV.

Spitting Image (2020) Trump's arsehole tweets from bed. *YouTube*, 1 Nov. Available from www.youtube.com/watch?v=A0c66bf-g1Q [accessed 24 January 2024].

Spitting Image Productions (1991) *Press Release: New Management Structure for Spitting Image*. Roger Law Collection, File Add.10275/4/53. Cambridge: Cambridge University Library.

Spitting Image Productions (undated a) *Spitting Images Brochure (on Licencing Opportunities)*. Roger Law Collection: File GBR/0012/MS Add.10275/4/32. Cambridge: Cambridge University Library.

Spitting Image Productions (undated b) *From a Frog to a Prince (Pamphlet to Promote Puppet 'Personal Appearances')*. Roger Law Collection, File GBR/0012/MS Add.10275/4/53. Cambridge: Cambridge University Library.

Spitting in Russian (2010) (radio) BBC Radio 4, 1 January, 1100.

Stier, S., Mangold, F., Scharkow, M. and Breuer, J. (2022) Post Post-Broadcast Democracy? News Exposure in the Online Intermediaries. *American Political Science Review*, 11(2), 768–74.

Stott, A. (2005) *Comedy*. Abingdon: Routledge.

Streicher, L.H. (1967) On a Theory of Political Caricature. *Comparative Studies*

in Society and History, 9(4) 427–45.
Sweney, M. (2020) Spitting Image to return after 24 years via BritBox. *The Guardian*, 4 March. Available from www.theguardian.com/media/2020/mar/04/spitting-image-to-return-after-24-years-via-britbox [accessed 31 January 2024].
Teste di gomma (1987–8) [television] TMC.
That Was the Week That Was (1962–3) [television] BBC Television.
This Morning (2016) [television] ITV. 27 September 2016, 11.30.
Thompson, A. (2021) *Blackface*. London and New York: Bloomsbury Press.
Thompson, M. (2021) *The Fruit of the Spirit is Love (Galatians 5:22)*. Available from https://poetrysociety.org.uk/poems/the-fruit-of-the-spirit-is-love-galatians-522 [accessed 19 February 2024].
The Times (1967) BBC asked to ban the TV minstrels. *The Times*, 19 May, 3.
The Times (1986) TV top ten. *The Times*, 9 April, 20.
The Times (1994) Top people's television. *The Times*, 18 May, 22.
Titley, G. (2019) *Racism and Media*. London: SAGE.
Top of the Pops (1964–2022) [television] BBC.
Uborka (1991–2002) [television] Magyar Televízió.
Vernon, P. (2019) Craig David Interview. *The Times Magazine*, 19 July, 31–45.
Wafa, N. (2020) The Fruit of the Spirit Is Love (Galatians 5:22) by Marvin Thompson. *The Poetry Society*. Available at https://resources.poetrysociety.org.uk/wp-content/uploads/2021/06/21-poetryclass-NPC-resource-Wafa-Thompson.pdf [accessed 13 February 2024].
Wagg, S. (1992) You've Never Had It So Silly: The Politics of British Satirical Comedy From Beyond the Fringe to Spitting Image. In Dominic Strinati and Stephen Wagg (eds) *Come On Down? Popular Media Culture in Post-War Britain*. London: Routledge, 254–84.
Wall, N. (2020) Who could possibly be offended by this toothless series of Spitting Image? *The Independent*, 8 October. Available from www.independent.co.uk/voices/spitting-image-britbox-boris-johnson-michael-gove-priti-patel-puppets-b886769.html [accessed 31 January 2024].
Waller, M. (1990) New face at Spitting Image. *The Times*, 22 January, 23.
Wanzo, R. (2020) *The Content of Our Caricature: African American Comic Art and Political Belonging*. New York: NYU Press.
Weaver, S. (2011) *The Rhetoric of Racist Humour: US, UK and Global Race Joking*. Farnham: Ashgate.
Wechsler, J. (1983) The Issue of Caricature. *Art Journal*, 43(4) 317–18.
Whannel, G. (2000) The Lads and the Gladiators: Traditional Masculinities in a Postmodern Televisual Landscape. In: E. Buscombe (ed.) *British Television: A Reader*. Oxford: Clarendon Press, 290–302.
What a F***in Year on TV with Mel B and Mel B (2019) [television] E4. 17

December 2019, 21.00.
Who Do You Do? (1972–6) [television] LWT.
Williams, Z. (2016) Is satire dead? Armando Iannucci and others on why there are so few laughs these days. *The Guardian*, 18 October. Available from www.theguardian.com/culture/2016/oct/18/is-satire-dead-politicians-held-in-contempt-armando-iannucci-few-laughs [accessed 12 March 2024].
Wilson, B. (2020) Spitting Image creator Roger Law on bringing satire to Britbox as he reveals what he really thinks of Boris. *Radio Times*, 3 October. Available from www.radiotimes.com/tv/comedy/spitting-image-roger-law-britbox-big-rt-interview [accessed 31 January 2024].
The Windsors (2016–) [television] Channel 4, series 1–4.
The Winjin' Pom (1991) [television] ITV.
Wollaston, S. (2022) It's a song about losing! Skinner, Baddiel and Broudie on 26 years of Three Lions – and bringing it up to date. *The Guardian*, 20 November. Available from www.theguardian.com/lifeandstyle/2022/nov/20/its-a-song-about-losing-skinner-baddiel-and-broudie-on-26-years-of-three-lions-and-bringing-it-up-to-date [accessed 1 March 2024].
Yeates, C. (2020) Spitting Image fires back at racism complaints and insists 'big noses and ears is personal'. *Metro*, 29 September. Available from https://metro.co.uk/2020/09/29/spitting-image-fires-back-at-racism-complaints-and-insists-big-noses-and-ears-is-personal-13342225 [accessed 22 March 2024].
Young, R. (1992) Cost-cutting tourists bypass the Tower. *The Times*, 2 November, 5.
Zheng, R. and Stear, N. (2023) Imagining in Oppressive Contexts, or What's Wrong with Blackface? *Ethics*, 133(3) 381–414.

Index

2DTV, 86
30 Rock, 140

AbsoluteLee Podcast, 129, 131
Action News, 51
address, 17, 19–20, 21–31, 34, 39–40, 42, 44–9, 53, 55–6, 61–2, 75, 111, 117, 124, 130, 137, 139, 144, 147, 150–2, 156–7; *see also* disposition
animation, 5, 8, 8n, 17, 20, 32–48, 51, 61, 86, 90, 150, 152, 154
antiracism, 95–6, 108, 138, 141
antisemitism, 96, 129–32, 145
audience, 11, 13, 16, 20, 21–6, 29, 34, 39–40, 42, 46, 48, 50, 53–4, 55–7, 59, 61–2, 66, 77–9, 86, 89–90, 94, 96, 101–3, 105–6, 111, 113–14, 122, 124–5, 137, 139, 142–3, 144, 148, 151, 156
Avalon, 87, 91–2, 101–2

Baddiel and Skinner Unplanned, 131
Baddiel, David, 84, 109, 121–32, 145
Baldwin, Alec, 44–6
BBC, 55, 67, 69, 85, 88–9, 112–14, 128–9, 143
BBC Three, 55
Bell, Steve, 20, 36, 57
Big Brother, 137
Big Brother's Little Brother, 137

The Black and White Minstrel Show, 107, 112–15, 118, 143
blackface, 18, 106, 107–46, 148
  blackface minstrelsy, 112–15
Black Lives Matter, 95–7, 108, 140
Blair, Jon, 68, 70, 74, 84
Blair, Tony, 38–40
BoJack Horseman, 32
Bo Selecta, 109, 131, 133–40, 145, 149–50
Brass Eye, 137–8
Broadcasters Audience Research Board (BARB), 78, 101, 137
Bremner, Rory, 40
Bremner, Bird and Fortune, 40
Britbox, 17, 66, 88–90, 94, 96, 100–2, 104
Brown, Faith, 31, 41
Brown, Janet, 31
Brown, Melanie, 133–4, 140

cancellation, 100, 102, 108, 109, 142, 145; *see also* political correctness, wokeness
caricature
  caricature signature, 9, 16, 24, 30, 42–3, 50, 58, 63, 120, 123, 148
  caricature paradox, 5–6, 10, 15, 46, 147; *see also* distorted recognition

caricature (*cont.*)
  caricaturist, 7–9, 16, 25, 31, 36, 66, 70, 72, 153
  history of, 1–2, 4–5, 7, 77, 117
  political caricature, 1–2, 9–12, 32, 39–40, 44, 58, 66, 100, 104, 152–3, 155; *see also* satire
  queer caricature, 21, 55–61
  racist caricature, 18, 27, 96, 109, 116–17, 121, 123, 131–2, 135–6, 142–3, 145; *see also* racism
  see also cartoon
cartoon, 5, 9n, 20, 22–3, 25–6, 34, 36, 39, 57
censorship, 28, 74, 87, 95, 100, 103, 105, 110, 139, 140–2
Central Independent Television, 17, 69–74, 77–8, 84, 90, 104–5
Channel 4, 36, 39–40, 67, 69, 109, 126, 129, 137–8, 140, 142
Channel 4 News, 36
Chipz, Baga, 56–7, 59–60
citizenship, 2–3, 20, 27–9, 47, 61–2, 120, 149, 151, 157
CNN, 34
comedy, 13–14, 15, 28, 67, 73, 77–8, 87, 90, 91–2, 95, 102, 107, 109, 110–11, 129, 133, 136–7, 139–40, 155; *see also* humour
  political comedy, 14, 28, 40, 90, 99, 102
  satirical comedy, 28; *see also* satire
  sitcom, 20, 32–4, 36, 43, 45, 48, 68, 70, 90, 92, 112
  sketch comedy, 32, 41–48, 53, 61, 63–4, 68, 70, 73, 84, 91–2, 102, 109, 133, 155
comic public sphere, 2, 10, 28–9, 31, 40, 46–7, 62, 149, 151, 156–7; *see also* public sphere
compliance, 94–5, 139

conservatism, 6, 12–13, 47, 55, 86–7, 95–6, 105, 109–10, 147
COVID-19, 91, 97, 153
Crossroads, 72
culture wars, 87, 95–6, 99, 105–6, 109–10, 139, 142, 148; *see also* cancel culture, political correctness, wokeness
cultural public sphere, 3, 17, 20, 28, 39, 62, 74, 76, 114, 120, 128, 131–2, 139, 144–5, 147, 151, 156; *see also* public sphere
Curry and Chips, 112
Cutting Edge: Footballers' Wives, 126–8

David Baddiel: Jews Don't Count, 129–32
David, Craig, 133–6, 138, 145, 149, 153
David Harewood on Blackface, 143
Dead Ringers, 11, 41
deepfakes, 154–6
Deepfake Neighbour Wars, 155
demographics
  ABC1, 11, 39, 79, 151
  young people, 11, 57, 78, 137, 139, 151
Denton, Charles, 69, 73–4, 76–8, 90
Di Domenico, John, 51–3
dignity, 118–19, 125–6, 140n, 149
disposition, 20, 25–6, 30, 47, 58, 61–2, 124, 144; *see also* address
distorted recognition, 6, 16, 23, 26, 33–4, 62, 94, 104, 147
Doctor Who, 43
drag, 54–9
Drunk History UK, 124

exaggeration, 5–10, 12, 15–16, 19, 30–1, 33, 41, 43–4, 54–5, 58,

60–2, 87, 113, 116, 120–1, 131, 147, 149–50, 152–5

Fantasy Football League, 109, 121–6, 130, 139, 142, 150
Fluck, Peter, 66–8, 71, 74, 80
Fox News, 33–4
Francis, Leigh, 109, 131, 133–6, 140, 145, 149
The Fruit of the Spirit is Love (Galatians 5:22), 120–1, 123, 125, 128
Futurama, 91

gaze, 1, 3–4, 22–3, 148
Gillray, James, 1–3
glance, 4, 22–3, 25, 40, 50, 148
Goddard, Trisha, 133–6
Gomez, Michelle, 41–3
Gone With the Wind, 143
Good Morning Britain, 48–9
Grant, Rob, 70, 81
Green Wing, 43
The Guardian, 36, 40

Headcases, 86
Hendra, Tony, 67–8, 70, 74
Hislop, Ian, 73
homophobia, 95, 124
Horrible Histories, 124
humour, 6, 12–14, 33, 43–4, 47, 55, 60, 75, 91–4, 95, 102–3, 105, 110–11, 118–20, 124, 133, 135; *see also* comedy
  ethics 110–11
  politics 109–10, 124
  theories, 12–14

ideology, 22, 26–7, 38–9, 44, 47, 103, 111, 116–18, 124, 131–2
The Imitation Game, 8

immediacy, 2, 11, 20, 23, 25, 29–30, 40, 41, 48, 99, 102, 104, 147, 151
impersonation, 4, 5, 8, 17–18, 19–21, 24–5, 31, 35, 40, 41, 44, 46–7, 48, 51–4, 55–6, 58–9, 61, 74, 107n, 111, 113, 116, 121, 132, 133–4, 144, 153, 155, 157
impression, 8, 17, 30, 36, 41, 43–4, 49, 52, 54, 56, 58, 61, 72–3, 81, 109, 133–4
The Impressions Show, 41
Independent Broadcasting Authority (IBA), 69, 70, 73–4, 77–9, 85, 94, 105
individuation, 1, 5, 6–9, 10, 14, 16, 105–6, 113, 116, 120, 134, 144–5, 147–8
irony, 25, 37–8, 40, 42, 49, 75–6, 80–1, 110, 124, 132, 133, 144–5, 149, 155
ITV, 39, 48–9, 52, 67, 69, 77–9, 85–6, 88–90, 96, 99, 100–1, 155
ITVX, 100–1

Jews Don't Count, 129–32, 145
Johnson, Boris, 87, 92, 97–8, 100, 102

lad culture, 123–4, 132
The Late Show with Stephen Colbert, 33
Law, Roger, 66–8, 71, 74, 80–1, 84, 87, 90, 96–7, 102–3, 104
Lee, Jason, 109, 121–32, 136, 142, 145
Les Guignols de l'info, 83
Lipman, Maureen, 31
Little Britain, 140
Lloyd, John, 67–8, 70, 73–4, 76, 81, 84, 93

Margaret Thatcher: Where Am I Now?, 20, 36–40, 42, 57
The Mary Whitehouse Experience, 84
The Melting Pot, 112
merchandise, 17, 80–2, 84, 137
MTV, 81

Nallon, Steve, 49–50, 54, 63, 72
Naylor, Doug, 70, 73, 81
Netflix, 89–90, 94, 101
Newman, Nick, 73
Newzoids, 86
Not the Nine O'clock News, 68, 81

Ofcom, 94, 101
offence, 14, 35, 79, 92, 95–6, 99, 103, 105–6, 109–10, 114, 118, 125, 135–6, 139, 141–2, 144–5, 157
Omnibus: Luck and Flaw's Illustrated Guide to Caricature, 71
Our Cartoon President, 20, 33–6, 40, 53

Patriot Act with Hasan Minhaj, 90
Peak TV, 66, 88–9, 93
physiognomy, 7, 12, 55, 63, 113, 116–17, 154
political correctness, 95, 99, 109, 110, 124, 133, 139, 142, 145; *see also* cancellation, wokeness
postmodernism, 124, 133, 145
The Problem with Jon Stewart, 90
Psychobitches, 20, 41–4, 47, 57, 149
public sphere, 2–3, 16, 27–8, 62, 114, 119–20, 126, 132, 144, 149, 156–7; *see also* comic public sphere, cultural public sphere

racism, 27, 95, 108, 109–20, 123–4, 128–32, 136, 140–3, 145
Ravens, Jan, 72, 86
Reagan, Ronald, 63, 81

reboot, 86, 88–90; *see also Spitting Image* Reboot (2020–1)
Robbins, Kate, 54, 72
Robinson, Morgana, 41
Rory Bremner, Who Else, 40
royal family, 72, 74–7, 79, 96, 100, 103, 105
RuPaul's Drag Race, 54–6
RuPaul's Drag Race UK, 21, 55–9

Sassy Justice with Fred Sassy, 154–5
satire, 2, 5–6, 9–12, 16, 17, 18, 25–6, 28, 33–5, 36, 38, 41, 46–7, 55–7, 59–61, 63–4, 66, 68, 73, 77, 84, 87, 91–2, 97, 99, 102, 104–5, 109, 117–20, 125, 133, 137, 141, 144, 148–9, 152–4, 156; *see also* political comedy
Saturday Night Live, 12, 20, 44–7
Scarfe, Gerald, 57
Scrubs, 140
sexism, 72, 95, 116, 124, 134
showtime, 20, 34
The Silence of the Lambs, 41–2
silly citizenship, 28–9, 61, 157
The Simpsons, 32–3, 91
Skinner, Frank, 109, 121, 123, 126, 128–9, 131
Sky Arts, 20, 41
social media, 93, 99, 101–2, 108–9, 130, 132, 133, 136, 146, 150, 153–3
South Park, 32, 154
Spitting Image, 17, 49, 63–106, 107, 137, 148–52, 155
  original series (1984–96), 66–86
  reboot (2020–1), 87–100
  Spitting Image: Idiots Assemble, 102–4
stereotype, 7, 96, 105–6, 116, 118, 120, 132, 134–5, 143, 144–5, 147–8, 157

streaming, 66, 88–90, 100, 109
Subscription Video on Demand (SVOD), 29, 89–90, 94, 100–1, 151–2
subversion, 6, 10, 12–13, 39, 41, 43, 55, 58, 60–1, 111, 118, 144–5, 147, 154

television
  archive, 18, 108–9, 132, 140–2, 145, 148
  broadcasting, 3n, 11, 21–2, 27, 29–30, 39, 45, 48, 50, 66–9, 85, 94n, 101–2, 104–5, 109, 137, 140, 142, 150–2, 156–7
  export, 83, 94, 105
  industry, 4, 11, 16–18, 22–3, 29, 39–40, 64–6, 67, 83, 85–6, 88–90, 93–4, 96 104–6, 128, 136, 141–3, 147, 150–1, 156–7
  in the 1980s, 49–51, 63–86
  in the 1990s, 38–40, 84–86, 121–9
  in the 2000s, 133–40
  in the 2020s, 86–102, 151
  narrowcasting, 29, 41, 54
  on-demand, 3n, 17, 23, 29–30, 66, 89, 93, 101–2, 105, 140, 151 157
  post-broadcast television, 29, 150
  regulation, 28–9, 69, 70, 73–5, 85, 94, 96, 104–5, 139, 148
  schedule, 11, 30, 33, 39, 41, 62, 77, 100, 113, 137, 151
  television Studies, 4, 17, 20–3, 26, 64
Teste di gomma, 83

Thatcher, Margaret, 17, 19–20, 31–2, 36–40, 41–4, 49–51, 56–7, 59–60, 61, 63–4, 71–2, 81–2, 85, 98, 148–9
That Was the Week That Was, 77
The Times, 78, 79, 84, 92
This Morning, 52
Thompson, Marvin, 109, 120–2, 128, 132
Thunberg, Greta, 92, 96
Today, 52
topicality, 9, 11, 25, 33, 50, 70, 73, 80, 90, 101, 103, 104–5, 148, 152
Top of the Pops, 81, 82
Tracey Breaks the News, 12
Trump, Donald, 17, 19–20, 31–2, 33–5, 44–7, 51–3, 56, 58–61, 87–8, 92, 100, 103, 149, 154–5

Uborka, 84

Very Slippy Weather, 1–2, 4
Video on Demand (VOD), 17, 29, 66, 89–90, 93, 101, 140, 152
The Vivienne, 58–60

What a F***in Year on TV with Mel B and Mel B, 140
Who Do You Do?, 41
The Windsors, 11
The Winjin' Pom, 84, 86
wokeness, 94–100, 103, 105, 107, 142; see *also* cancel culture, culture wars, political correctness

Yarwood, Mike, 41

EU representative:
Easy Access System Europe
Mustamäe tee 50, 10621 Tallinn, Estonia
Gpsr.requests@easproject.com

www.ingramcontent.com/pod-product-compliance
Lightning Source LLC
Chambersburg PA
CBHW051127160426
43195CB00014B/2378